Robert J. Bonk, PhD

Medical Writing in Drug Development
A Practical Guide for Pharmaceutical Research

Pre-publication
REVIEWS,
COMMENTARIES,
EVALUATIONS . . .

"**C**omprehensive and exceptionally well-organized, Robert Bonk's new book will serve as an outstanding resource for practitioners and students alike. The range of coverage is impressive: from regulatory writing and audience analysis to the rhetorical strategy for publications and the ethical responsibilities of biomedical writers. Bonk covers all of the salient points effectively and without excess. The templates for clinical trial reports, an overview regulatory document, and a publication manuscript should prove to be valuable to all professionals."

William T. Walker, PhD
Associate Dean, Arts and Sciences;
Chair, Department of Humanities,
Philadelphia College of Pharmacy
and Science

More pre-publication
REVIEWS, COMMENTARIES, EVALUATIONS . . .

"This brief, well-organized book offers students a helpful introduction to pharmaceutical writing. It can also be of use to others wishing to explore this field. The appendixes and some of the tables seem especially helpful.

In short, this book helps fill an important niche. It is a welcome addition to my medical-writing bookshelf."

Barbara Gastel, MD
Associate Professor of Journalism and Medical Humanities;
Coordinator, MS Program in Science and Technology Journalism, Texas A&M University

"Dr. Bonk describes his book as a 'working map' for the craft of medical writing. He has usefully divided this working map into three equally important parts. The overview of pharmaceutical research in the first part of the book gives the context in which to understand the role and skill of the medical writer. The different types of documents that form regulatory submissions are described in the second part and this account enables the reader to appreciate the challenges these documents present to medical writing. The different requirements for publication documents are given in the third part of the book and, here, it is refreshing to see the author give a frank discussion of ethical issues and the medical writer's responsibilities for these persuasive documents.

For medical writers new to the profession, this book is a valuable, practical guide. Skilled medical writers will recognize that the author has a wealth of professional experience; his breadth of knowledge and his views will be appreciated.

With pleasing clarity, Bonk offers medical writers sound, practical advice and guidance on present-day and future challenges to the profession."

Jane Mitchell, DPhil
Medical Writing Services, Staffordshire, England

The Pharmaceutical Products Press
An Imprint of the Haworth Press, Inc.

Medical Writing
in Drug Development
A Practical Guide
for Pharmaceutical Research

THE PHARMACEUTICAL PRODUCTS PRESS
Pharmaceutical Sciences
Mickey C. Smith, PhD
Executive Editor

New, Recent, and Forthcoming Titles:

Principles of Pharmaceutical Marketing edited by Mickey C. Smith

Pharmacy Ethics edited by Mickey C. Smith, Steven Strauss, John Baldwin, and Kelly T. Alberts

Drug-Related Problems in Geriatric Nursing Home Patients by James W. Cooper

Pharmaceutical Marketing: Strategy and Cases by Mickey C. Smith

International Pharmaceutical Services: The Drug Industry and Pharmacy Practice in Twenty-Three Major Countries of the World edited by Richard N. Spivey, Albert I. Wertheimer, and T. Donald Rucker

A Social History of the Minor Tranquilizers: The Quest for Small Comfort in the Age of Anxiety by Mickey C. Smith

Marketing Pharmaceutical Services: Patron Loyalty, Satisfaction, and Preferences edited by Harry A. Smith and Joel Coons

Nicotine Replacement: A Critical Evaluation edited by Ovide F. Pomerleau and Cynthia S. Pomerleau

Herbs of Choice: The Therapeutic Use of Phytomedicinals by Varro E. Tyler

Interpersonal Communication in Pharmaceutical Care by Helen Meldrum

Searching for Magic Bullets: Orphan Drugs, Consumer Activism, and Pharmaceutical Development by Lisa Ruby Basara and Michael Montagne

The Honest Herbal by Varro E. Tyler

Understanding the Pill: A Consumer's Guide to Oral Contraceptives by Greg Juhn

Pharmaceutical Chartbook, Second Edition edited by Abraham G. Hartzema and C. Daniel Mullins

The Handbook of Psychiatric Drug Therapy for Children and Adolescents by Karen A. Theesen

Children, Medicines, and Culture edited by Patricia J. Bush, Deanna J. Trakas, Emilio J. Sanz, Rolf L. Wirsing, Tuula Vaskilampi, and Alan Prout

Social and Behavioral Aspects of Pharmaceutical Care edited by Mickey C. Smith and Albert I. Wertheimer

Studies in Pharmaceutical Economics edited by Mickey C. Smith

Drugs of Natural Origin: Economic and Policy Aspects of Discovery, Development, and Marketing by Anthony Artuso

Pharmacy and the U.S. Health Care System, Second Edition edited by Jack E. Fincham and Albert I. Wertheimer

Medical Writing in Drug Development: A Practical Guide for Pharmaceutical Research by Robert J. Bonk

Medical Writing
in Drug Development
A Practical Guide
for Pharmaceutical Research

Robert J. Bonk, PhD

The Pharmaceutical Products Press
An Imprint of The Haworth Press, Inc.
New York • London

Published by

The Pharmaceutical Products Press, an imprint of The Haworth Press, Inc., 10 Alice Street, Binghamton, NY 13904-1580

Cover design by Marylouise E. Doyle.

Library of Congress Cataloging-in-Publication Data

Bonk, Robert J.
  Medical writing in drug development : a practical guide for pharmaceutical research / Robert J. Bonk.
    p.   cm.
  Includes bibliographical references and index.
  ISBN 0-7890-0449-6 (alk. paper).
    1. Drugs—Research. 2. Medical writing. I. Title. [DNLM: 1. Writing. 2. Publishing. 3. Drug Approval. 4. Research. WZ 345 B714m 1997]
RM301.25.B66 1997
808'.066615—dc21

                                                                97-18243
                                                                CIP

To friends, who never tire of listening;

and

to family, who never tire of answering.

ABOUT THE AUTHOR

Robert J. Bonk, PhD, has an eclectic background that reflects many facets of the field of medical writing. A noted professional in this area, he worked for nearly two decades in the pharmaceutical industry, most recently as Manager of Medical Communications for an international firm. In this role, he directed a diverse staff who encompassed the related areas of medical writing, technical editing, and electronic publishing. In close collaboration with international colleagues, Dr. Bonk developed electronic publishing systems that have been presented in public forums. Complementing his professional role, Dr. Bonk has maintained strong academic affiliations. In fact, he now holds positions of Adjunct Associate Professor at the Philadelphia College of Pharmacy and Science and in the University of Delaware's English Department.

Underpinning Dr. Bonk's practical experience are educational credentials that span both the writing and scientific fields. These include a BA with Highest Honors in Biology and Chemistry from the University of Delaware; an MS in Technical and Science Communication from Drexel University; and a PhD in Pharmacy Administration from the Philadelphia College of Pharmacy and Science. Active both locally and nationally in the American Medical Writers Association (AMWA), he is a former recipient of the AMWA Certificate in Pharmaceutical Writing.

CONTENTS

Figures

Chapter 11

Chapter 12

Chapter 13

Chapter 14

Tables

Chapter 9

Chapter 12

Chapter 14

Foreword

A decade ago (spring of 1987), I had a student in my graduate course in "Writing and Publishing Scientific Papers" named Robert J. Bonk. He was already a seasoned medical-writing professional at that time, so it was no surprise that he was the star of the class during that term. And he *was* the star, and I have since watched this rising star as his career has moved ever forward. Now, he is not only a medical writer of note; he has been an administrator of a large group of medical writers in an important pharmaceutical house, and he is also a teacher of scientific (pharmaceutical) writing here at the University of Delaware, as well as at the Philadelphia College of Pharmacy and Science.

So it is time that Dr. Bonk wrote a book. Not just a book, but *the* book, the definitive book on writing in the pharmaceutical field. And he has done just that. His book is brimming with sage instruction and advice that will be of inestimable use to both beginning and seasoned writers in the pharmaceutical field.

What I find most satisfying about Dr. Bonk's book is its logical organization. The reader can move from chapter to chapter in an almost seamless learning process. Note, for example, how the book starts out. Chapter 1 is titled "Basic Introduction to Medical Writing," as it should be. Chapter 2 satisfyingly moves to "Overview of Drug Development." Chapter 3 then begins the reader's exploration of more specific subjects, discussing "Types of Pharmaceutical Documents." Chapter 4, "Professional Roles of Medical Writers," introduces the cast of characters. Chapter 5 then grabs us by the ears and makes us look at our present and our immediate future in a powerhouse chapter titled "Publishing and Information Technology." These five chapters are the first of three parts of the book. The chapters in all three parts of the book follow in the same logical flow, each building on the solid foundation of the preceding chapter. Such logicality makes the learning process both easy and enjoyable.

"It was a dark and stormy night." Everyone who has ever written a book knows that the first sentence is the hardest to write. Perhaps this reflects that the first sentence often sets the tone for all that follow. A dull first sentence is likely a harbinger of woes to come. A sharp first sentence can grab the reader's attention and interest, leading the way into a useful book. Here is Dr. Bonk's first sentence: "Information explodes around us through our modern technology, and perhaps nowhere more than in health care." Doesn't that profound sentence pique your interest? Of course it does. Therefore, I now end this foreword so that you can quickly move on and read Dr. Bonk's first sentence, and his second, and all the rest. I'll bet the traditional dollar to a day-old doughnut that you will enjoy this book. I know that I did.

Robert A. Day
University of Delaware

Preface

In 1995, I first began discussions with professors at the University of Delaware about a personal quest: the development of a college-level course on pharmaceutical writing. No one could argue about the time being right; along the east coast's healthcare corridor, what topic could be more geographically suited? So, with the encouragement and support of these fine academicians of the University's program in Business and Technical Writing, I developed my course syllabus and related materials.

Never having designed a complete course of my own, I relished the challenge. Direct professional experience with my medical-writing associates—including those within the American Medical Writers Association—made this task somewhat less daunting. My greatest surprise, though, was the lack of one foundation text spanning the areas of medical writing for drug development. So I decided to write my own; here it is!

Another challenge in writing this book concerned the field's breadth, with new medical discoveries changing our approaches to health care, new burgeoning computerization becoming the tool of our trade, and new audiences eager to hear new messages. The strand to bridge the diversity of pharmaceutical writing charted my book's structure: this book's three parts encompass strategies and techniques key to preparing documents for drug development.

With a clear perspective on medical writing, Part I overviews drug research, document types, professional roles, and information technology. Part II delineates those regulatory documents that comprise drug submissions, stressing commonalities and differences across research reports, summary documents, and supportive materials. Part III highlights external publications for the medical community, developing rhetorical strategies for journal manuscripts, conference materials, and promotional pieces, complemented by issues currently reshaping the healthcare arena.

Through each part and its component chapters, this book leads medical writers and their associates—scientific, regulatory, and marketing professionals—to a working knowledge of those technical documents on which successful drug research depends. This book also provides a foundation text for biomedical-writing courses. Thus, I hope that you, the reader, find that I, the author, tailored a book to fit the library niche that I discovered in 1995.

Acknowledgments

This book—my first—would not have been possible without caring support of family, friends, and colleagues. Professor Robert A. Day, who always encouraged my writing, deserves special recognition, as do his associates at the University of Delaware.

As a writer, I know the value of technical expertise for editing and graphics. For these respective services on my book, I thank Angie Piccoli and Tracy Naughton. Their friendship has been an extra bonus during this process.

Introductory quotations for each chapter originated from the 1995 and 1996 editions of "The Book Lovers' Calendar" by Elizabeth Hill and Martha Starr of Starhill Press. For a book lover such as myself, what could be more inspiring day to day?

And to the American Medical Writers Association (AMWA), the best professional group for those practicing my craft, I extend a hearty handshake for fostering in me the skill and knowledge that can lead all of us to shape the future of medical writing.

PART I:
MEDICAL WRITING
FOR PHARMACEUTICAL RESEARCH

Medical writing attracts a diverse group of professionals, ranging from communications specialists to laboratory scientists to health-care practitioners. To establish common ground for this wide audience, Part I spotlights medical writing within the context of a general overview of pharmaceutical research.

Chapter 1

Basic Introduction to Medical Writing

The author should be like God in the universe,
present everywhere but in no way visible.

—Gustave Flaubert

Information explodes around us through our modern technology, and perhaps nowhere more than in health care. Recent scientific and biotechnological advances amplify our understanding of health and disease, often fortuitously with new treatment modalities. But, to be of any practical use, these advances must also be communicated to those who can use and benefit from them. New information technologies facilitate quick communication, yet confusion can also reign during information overload. How can this information burden be juggled effectively? And to our advantage?

Through healthcare communicators: specifically "medical writers" who capture, meld, disentangle, juxtapose, and reassemble biomedical information into logical packages for varied audiences. This book explores the role of medical writers in the healthcare communication process, with a particular focus on the development of new drugs.

HISTORICAL ROOTS
OF HEALTHCARE COMMUNICATION

During these past several decades of technological advancement, medical writing has emerged as a pivotal profession in the health-care arena, particularly in the research and development of new pharmaceutical products. Paradoxically for health care, many breakthroughs developed from the carnage of war. For example, new treatments emerging from the horrors of World War II included penicillin and other antibiotics for combating infectious diseases, surgical procedures for complex multiple injuries, and psychological approaches for the emotional and mental devastation of shell shock and other disturbances (Watts, 1987).

While of value in and of themselves for the wartime soldiers, these medical advances captured a watershed moment in history as the launching pad for more sophisticated accomplishments in health care. But this fertile ground would remain barren if the information of these advances were never communicated. Not only do researchers and academicians rely on timely dissemination of scientific knowledge to feed further study, but the public needs the information to drive government and corporate support for additional advances in healthcare technology.

Much of this advancement stems from the transformation of the practice of medicine during this century: our parents and grandparents may have unquestionably accepted the physician's diagnosis, but today we may challenge this diagnosis, or at least want to learn more about our own health condition. Modern technology quickly provides us information about health, but safeguards about correct interpretation and appropriate dissemination of this key information are crucial to its effective use (Berland, 1983).

Who serves this pivotal role in healthcare communication? The medical writer. The profession of scientific or technical writing, of which medical writing is a key specialty, responded to the critical need to handle the burgeoning technological information from this historical era (Losi, 1987). The information itself grew disproportionate to the ability of its generators, the scientists, to handle it directly. Hence, writers and other information specialists became the communicators and custodians of these data so that scientists could focus on substance, thereby generating more advances. And, in some respects, medical writers became translators of this information, ensuring that correct messages would be received and understood by intended audiences, whether technical wizards, interested laypersons, or someone intermediate in perspective.

SOCIAL FABRIC OF MEDICAL WRITING

The power of the medical writer, of course, depends in large part on the information source: healthcare information is vital to everyone at some, if not all, stages of their own lives and those of their families. Moreover, because communication is a social phenomenon, the medical writer exerts indirect influence on our cultural fabric, weaving a new rhetorical landscape across communication media (Bazerman, 1991).

These cultural effects of medical writing are also evidenced by changes in literary and artistic presentations of medical themes over the past few centuries (Bazerman, 1991). Consider just the overall look of medical textbooks from the previous few centuries, with hand-drawn graphics indicating the controlling powers of humours and herbs, potions and poultices. And now compare the detailed electron microscopy of modern medical textbooks. Then peruse the self-help area of any bookstore for a layperson's guide to health and disease, and note the depth of technical detail. Moreover, while themes of health and disease populate our literary heritage from ancient times, no one can deny the keen interest of today's public in medical books, videos, and talk shows.

Through their deft handling of this information, professional medical writers exert intended—and sometimes unintended—effects on our social milieu. Information lives and breathes within our complex cultural fabric. Through interplay with other aspects and institutions of society, presentation becomes interpretation. Medical writers can therefore transform the social reality of medicine (Bazerman, 1991).

PHARMACEUTICAL WRITING AT THE FOREFRONT

Given the increasing attention, in both public and private sectors, to the segment of health care that comprises pharmaceutical products (Bonk, Myers, and McGhan, 1995), the medical writer who specializes in drug development often commands a key role. Because drugs capture a small, but personally felt, piece of our own expenditures, the seemingly high prices for "magic bullets" to cure our ailments, or at least alleviate the symptoms, force the pharmaceutical field to the forefront of public and private scrutiny.

With this focused attention comes the need for careful handling of information related to drugs. This information spans wide vistas: technical details on scientific discovery; factual compilations to support government licensure for marketing; educational pieces for the medical community and, more commonly, the patient; and even advertising to keep healthcare practitioners aware of new advances. Thus, within this scope, the medical writer who specializes in the pharmaceutical discipline plays a pivotal role in healthcare provision.

Exploring this important role of the medical writer in communicating drug information, this book provides a practical guide for the new and not-so-new professional. Not a style guide, this book is a working map for the craft of medical writing.

Chapter 2

Overview of Drug Development

The circumstances for sustained creation are almost impossible.

—Tillie Olsen

"Take this antibiotic three times a day for ten days; don't stop because you feel better!" "Nurse, set up an IV drip for this oncologic agent; watch carefully for signs of nausea." "You need to take this medication every morning, to keep your blood pressure down."

Three very different scenarios for prescribing a drug. Yet, all three drugs would have passed through the same basic set of requirements for marketing approval from the Food and Drug Administration (FDA) in the United States, including types of regulatory documentation required for that approval. How can that be?

Understanding the pharmaceutical research and development process, with a special eye on the underlying documentation, is perforce a requisite of professional success in medical writing. Through deliberate focus, this overview clarifies main aspects of an operationally complex process, so that the rhetorical strategies detailed in subsequent chapters will gel for the medical writer.

REGULATION OF THE DRUG PROCESS

Several excellent references provide the source information for this delineation of the research and development process for a new prescription drug. These references include documents issued by the government for the typical consumer (Pines, 1981; U.S. Department of Health and Human Services, 1981), as well as comprehensive texts that target pharmaceutical scientists (Spilker and Cuatrecasas, 1990; Smith, 1992). Consult these guides, as appropriate, for further exploration of the steps in the drug development process, as overviewed in this chapter.

Each country (or group, such as the European Community) maintains a regulatory agency to govern the approval process that allows new drugs to be marketed for specified diseases or therapeutic indications. In the United States, this agency is the FDA. For simplicity, this chapter focuses on the drug development process as typical for the United States under FDA regulation. Other countries follow comparable guidelines, particularly with the move to harmonization of all international regulations for drug development (Nightingale, 1995; further discussed in Chapter 7, "Foundation Reports of Research Trials").

In the United States, the current drug regulations developed over this past century. Among key pieces of legislation are the Federal Food, Drug, and Cosmetic Act of 1938 that mandated demonstration of safety of drugs; and the 1962 Kefauver-Harris Amendments to the Federal Food, Drug, and Cosmetic Act that required evidence of efficacy along with safety, and also further strengthened the FDA's jurisdiction.

SEQUENCE OF DRUG DEVELOPMENT

Before being marketed, a new drug must proceed through a sequence of stages to define its pharmacology, safety, and efficacy. These aspects consider the mechanism of action for the drug; its tolerability and side effects in the target population; and its ability to combat the disease, or at least relieve its symptoms. The general sequence may be modified according to specific circumstances; for example, drugs for a serious disease without other remedy, such as AIDS (Acquired Immune Deficiency Syndrome), may have the development process greatly accelerated.

Generally, though, drugs proceed through the following developmental sequence, with the goal to eliminate unlikely candidates as early as possible (Figure 2.1):

1. Pharmacological screening of new drug candidates
2. Nonclinical testing in laboratory models or animals
3. Filing of IND (Investigational New Drug) Application
4. Clinical research in humans (Phases I, II, and III)
5. Filing of NDA (New Drug Application)
6. Postmarketing surveillance after approval (Phase IV)

FIGURE 2.1. Likelihood of Drug Success

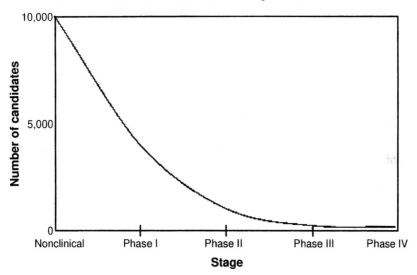

Time frames and costs for developing a new drug vary widely, depending on the severity of the disease to be treated, specific characteristics of the patient population, and even the difficulty of manufacturing the drug delivery system (e.g., oral tablet, aerosol spray, or intravenous infusion). Moreover, certain diseases, such as cancer, require years to determine if the drug works, whereas other conditions, such as a bacterial infection, may involve only weeks for comparable research. Still, overall timeframes equate to seven to twelve years for any new drug. Given pitfalls inherent in this risky venture of drug development, one can understand why only one of about every ten thousand potential candidates ever gets approved as a new drug! In parallel, estimated costs continue escalating, as researchers aim at diseases recalcitrant to current therapies (e.g., AIDS or certain cancers) or to more difficult patient populations (e.g., the elderly).

PHARMACOLOGICAL TESTING AND NONCLINICAL RESEARCH

Once a target disease has been identified, the development sequence commences. The earliest stages involve research into the chemistry, anatomy, and pharmacology of the target disease. This basic information allows the medicinal chemist and other scientists to design and synthesize potential drug candidates. These candidates must first pass a battery of pharmacological screening tests to elucidate the potential effects of this entity for the target disease. Additionally, in vitro tests with laboratory methods (not with animals) allow further information to be gleaned on the entity's safety.

With this valuable information, scientists whittle down the group of candidates to a select group with the greatest potential for efficacy, yet the lowest risk for safety. But since laboratory tests currently only simulate—not duplicate—the in vivo or living environment, nonclinical research with animals ensues. Such nonclinical research is conducted with the strictest adherence to FDA requirements so as to minimize the use of animals, and to ensure their humane treatment.

Because animal species can be closer to humans physiologically than are laboratory simulations, nonclinical research allows a closer look into the potential usefulness of the drug candidates. In addition to efficacy, nonclinical research identifies toxicological or other safety risks before a drug ever reaches the first human for testing. Moreover, animals metabolize the entity in manners analogous to humans. Thus, animal models allow researchers to estimate the appropriate dosage of a drug candidate for use in the first clinical trials in humans. Overall, this early research seeks to learn enough about the potential drug so that the initial group can be further pared down, with only the most likely candidates allowed to proceed into human testing.

FILING THE INVESTIGATIONAL NEW DRUG APPLICATION

Once sufficient pharmacological and nonclinical data have been gathered to support the likelihood of success for a drug candidate, the sponsor (usually a pharmaceutical company) requests FDA approval to begin clinical testing in humans. This strictly regulated process is initiated through the filing of an IND (Investigational New Drug) Application. Although enacted to allow interstate transfer of drugs not yet approved for marketing, the IND's central goal is to minimize risk to human subjects for clinical trials of new investigational drugs. To document this information, the IND Application includes five key components:

1. All available information on the drug (entity) and product (administered form)
2. Nonclinical data garnered from animal studies to support the drug's use
3. Investigator's Brochure that summarizes all such information to date
4. General plan of investigation for further research (for at least one year)
5. Protocol for the first clinical trial proposed for research in humans

The FDA reviewer assigned to this drug assesses the IND Application. Any questions or shortfalls are referred to the sponsor for solution. Unless notified by the FDA, the investigator can initiate the proposed clinical trial within thirty days of the IND filing.

PROTOCOLS FOR CLINICAL TRIALS

Although not always written (but typically reviewed and edited) by a medical writer, the protocol is a key foundation document for the subsequent clinical trial report (see Chapter 7, "Foundation Reports of Research Trials"). The protocol provides the basis, in terms of objectives and methods, for a clinical trial. Protocol design is beyond the scope of this book, but more information can be found in other references (Friedman, Furberg, and DeMets, 1984). Generally, each protocol contains at least the following major items:

- Clearly defined objectives (what specifically is the trial seeking to find out?)
- Criteria for inclusion and exclusion (which patients are being studied?)
- Drug dose and regimen (how is the drug administered, and at what strength?)
- Clinical versus pharmacological end points (how are results measured?)

- Definitions of success and failure (which results are considered meaningful?)
- Statistical design and analysis (how can data be reliably analyzed?)

This pivotal information, designed on a trial-by-trial basis, allows the investigator of a clinical trial to proceed in a scientific manner to learn more about the drug's actions in humans—yet continue to safeguard the human subjects enrolled in the trial.

FIRST THREE PHASES OF CLINICAL RESEARCH

Clinical research proceeds through "phases" of particular types of trials; only after a drug successfully functions in one phase does it progress to the next. The first three phases (I, II, and III) comprise the major trials that provide the basis on which a drug is approved (or not) for marketing. Table 2.1 compares the main features of these three phases, as discussed below.

TABLE 2.1. Comparative Features of Phases I, II, and III of Clinical Research

Feature	Phase I	Phase II	Phase III
Determination	Pharmacological activity, pharmacokinetics, and basic tolerance	Effective dose and regimen; early efficacy and safety information	Efficacy in main indication; rates of adverse events; and optimal dosage
Length	Short-term (single-dose or about ≤ 2 weeks)	Short-term dosing (about ≤ 2 months)	Longer-term, but depends on target disease
Size	Limited (≤ 10 subjects for each of ≤ 10 trials)	50 to 300 subjects (depends on trial design)	100s to 1,000s (depends on target disease)
Population	Healthy volunteers without the target disease for the drug candidate	Patients with the primary disease, but otherwise carefully restricted	Patients with the primary disease, with allowance for associated conditions

Phase I, the first phase of clinical research, determines the primary pharmacological activity, pharmacokinetic profile, and general tolerance of the drug in humans. These trials, by nature of the specific questions posed, are generally short-term (single-dose trials or dosing no more than about two weeks). Each trial may require only about ten or so subjects each, for perhaps about ten trials total, depending on the complexity of the drug's pharmacokinetic profile (i.e., its absorption through tissues, distribution among organs, metabolism by the liver, and excretion from the body). Because Phase I trials focus on basic understanding of the drug, these trials use healthy volunteers, rather than subjects with the target disease. That approach is saved for the second phase.

Phase II, the next phase of clinical research, determines the effective dose (strength) and regimen (how many times per day, and in what form) of the drug, along with early information on its efficacy and safety profiles. These trials typically involve short-term dosing (no more than about two months), in a total of approximately fifty to three hundred subjects (actual number being dependent on the trial design and target disease). In these trials, subjects are enrolled who have the primary target disease; however, additional complications (e.g., diabetes on top of hypertension) are restricted, so that the actions of the drug can be better understood before progressing to the third phase.

Phase III, the major phase of clinical research, is the final phase that gathers the bulk of information in humans to support government approval for marketing. These trials seek to demonstrate the efficacy of the drug for the primary indication or disease, its safety in terms of the rates of potential adverse events, and the optimal dosage in selected patient populations (e.g., children versus elderly). Both the length of a trial and the number of required subjects are disease-dependent: for example, oncology trials of cancer involve many subjects over several years to assess ability to lower mortality, whereas an analgesic to reduce headache may involve trials less complex in design. Generally, Phase III encompasses a range of subjects, numbering in the hundreds or sometimes the thousands, and may last for several years altogether. Because these trials focus on understanding the drug's true nature, subjects with the primary disease may be less restricted for associated conditions than in Phase II.

Assuming that results of this extensive clinical testing in Phases I, II, and III support the potential efficacy and safety of the drug candidate, the sponsor may next decide to file formally for approval to market the drug. This entails preparing an NDA.

OVERVIEW OF A NEW DRUG APPLICATION

The NDA, or New Drug Application, represents the culmination of all known nonclinical, clinical, and other knowledge about the drug, in support of FDA approval for marketing in the therapeutic indication and intended target population. Regulatory agencies of other countries require similar submissions, such as the NDS (New Drug Submission) in Canada, and the MAA (Marketing Approval Authorization) in Europe. The contents, though, of such regulatory submissions remain relatively constant in global terms, with components expected to reach increasing levels of harmonization (Nightingale, 1995). Such international consistency bodes well for pharmaceutical companies seeking more efficiency in drug development—and for medical writers who prepare major portions of NDA submissions and other regulatory documents!

In general terms, the NDA details all known information on the drug candidate, with presentation of this information in particular formats to facilitate agency review. The assigned FDA reviewer evaluates this information to judge the appropriateness to market this drug, as proposed by the sponsor. The main reviewer works in tandem with other technical experts at the FDA, who parcel specific components of the NDA for study. For example, a statistical expert reviews the statistics involved with the trials and analyses, whereas a chemist reviews details on drug formulation. (For additional details on the NDA, see Chapter 6, "Structure of Regulatory Submissions," and related chapters of Part II, "Regulatory Documents for Drug Submissions.")

Overall approval hinges on an acceptable ratio of potential risks to known benefits of the drug. The acceptable level of this ratio itself depends on the target condition: a higher level of side effects would be allowed for an oncologic medicine treating a recalcitrant cancer, but not for an antihypertensive when hypertension is treatable by alternative drugs. Such decisions on risk versus benefit of a new drug involve complex considerations of science, tempered by humanistic concern for the patient.

FOURTH PHASE OF CLINICAL RESEARCH

Although FDA approval allows the sponsor to market the new drug in the United States, the story of drug development—and the role of the medical writer—does not stop with the successful filing of an NDA. Throughout the earlier stages of development and beyond the NDA, medical writers contribute to promoting awareness of the drug in the wider medical community (see Part III, "Publication Documents for the Medical Community"). Moreover, the drug itself would next progress to the final phase.

Phase IV, an open-ended phase of clinical research, encompasses a variety of trials that seek to extend understanding of the new drug. Trials may be constructed to gain more knowledge of its actions in special patient populations (e.g., patients with renal impairment) or new conditions (e.g., mild rather than severe hypertension). Although these trials must still be scientifically sound, they may involve less rigor than in the pivotal trials of Phase III. (As an aside, trials initiated after the NDA is filed but before approval are termed "Phase IIIb" whereas those that are part of the NDA are "Phase IIIa.")

In some cases, the sponsor may wish to study the drug in wider circumstances. Would a drug for breast cancer, for example, also work in prostate cancer? Or might an antihypertensive also alleviate angina? If the new area of study is sufficiently different from the approved indication of the original NDA, such new trials may require a de facto return to Phases I, II, or III, instead of simply adding Phase IV trials.

Additionally, the sponsor is required to monitor safety and adverse events (i.e., side effects) of the drug as it is used more widely in the patient population. An adverse event occurring in 0.01 percent of the patients, for example, would require, in statistical terms, about 1,000 subjects for detection. Depending on the structure of the overall clinical program, such adverse events, or those occurring at lower rates, might not be caught before NDA filing. Postmarketing safety surveillance, as governed by FDA regulations, allows the sponsor to work with the FDA and the medical community, in ensuring the ultimate goal of drug development: the continued well-being of the patient, with minimal risks but maximal benefits from new therapies.

Chapter 3

Types of Pharmaceutical Documents

Only where there is language is there world.

—Adrienne Rich

Across all stages of drug development—from pharmacological and nonclinical studies to Phases I through IV of clinical research—a panoply of pharmaceutical documents emerges. But perhaps surprisingly, these varied documents generally partition into one of two main categories by audience analysis: first, regulatory documents that focus on government approval; second, publication documents that target the external medical community. This chapter distinguishes these two categories, identifies examples of specific documents, and discusses their rhetorical strategies.

ANALYSIS OF DOCUMENT AUDIENCES

Communication specialists commonly use audience analysis in designing documents to be understandable and usable by the intended recipient; otherwise, the documents would be worthless as information conduits. In the decoding of information imbedded within a particular document, many factors external to the document itself, but internal to the reader, influence that person's perception. Such factors contributing to selective perception include the reader's wants and needs for information, attitude toward the topic, and other psychological attributes (Severin and Tankard, 1988).

In the pressure-laden business of drug development, few researchers stop to consider how message coding indirectly and directly influences the reader's interpretation and use of key pharmaceutical information. Yet the medical writer for these assignments must understand the value of audience analysis, along with the other techniques of technical writing that contribute to comprehension. In fact, on the basis of intended audience, all of the pharmaceutical documents typically handled by medical writers fall into the two main classes of regulatory and publication documents. Keeping the audience in mind for each document type therefore facilitates the medical writer's role in maximizing information flow during drug development.

REGULATORY DOCUMENTS FOR DRUG SUBMISSIONS

Within the pharmaceutical industry, most writing tends to focus on those regulatory documents that form submissions to government or other agencies as part of the drug approval process (see Chapter 2, "Overview of Drug Development," for more details on this overall process). Since submissions detail the painstaking research conducted over years on a new potential drug, these regulatory documents are highly technical in nature. Often, the text portions of these documents contain imbedded tables and figures, supplemented by appended materials that can be text, tables, figures, images, or other output from modern technological sources. The specific type of regulatory document determines the content and structure of such components.

Among these varied types of regulatory documents, those most typically encountered by the medical writer include research reports for individual drug trials, overview documents that meld information across trials, and supportive materials that provide additional documentation (Table 3.1). The chapters of Part II delineate the actual construction of these types of regulatory documents. However, a broad introduction to these main types of regulatory documents follows.

Foundation reports of research trials (Chapter 7) detail the findings of each specific experimental study. Investigations into a drug's actions, efficacy, and safety form a series of discrete studies or trials, grouped by discipline. Early pharmacological and nonclinical research, for example, comprises many individual experiments in laboratory or animal settings. Similarly, each phase of clinical research involves a few to many individual trials under carefully controlled conditions in humans. Regardless of the type of research, each trial must be documented in terms of its objectives, methods, results, and conclu-

TABLE 3.1. Examples of Regulatory Documents

Type of regulatory document	Typical examples
Foundation reports of research trials	Nonclinical study report
	Phase III clinical trial report
Overviews and summary documents	Integrated summary of efficacy
	Integrated summary of safety
Supportive materials for drug submissions	List of clinical investigators
	Investigator's Brochure

sions, as well as for supplemental information (e.g., references) that support the trial as conducted. Formats for each report type depend on the research discipline, regulatory guidelines, and corporate requirements.

Overview and summary documents (Chapter 8) coalesce information from individual trials into a coherent picture for a specific intent. The overall efficacy profile of a new drug, for example, cannot be fully known without considering efficacy results from all trials that garnered such results; similarly, pharmacology, safety, and other attributes require information across various sources to be melded into a coherent view. Such information includes results of the same tests at different dosage levels, as well as of different tests that relate to various aspects of the drug's actions. Moreover, results from individual trials may agree, but could conflict; hence, their meshed interpretation pivotally determines the therapeutic profile of the new drug candidate.

Supportive materials for drug submissions (Chapter 9) provide additional information to supplement individual reports and overview documents. Often, regulatory guidelines for submissions drive the structure of such materials. Overview documents of drug submissions, for example, require tabulations of key aspects of methods, demography, and results for each group of trials. And each submission requires basic documents that summarize the drug's development strategy, highlight meetings with regulatory agencies on key decision points, and even list all of the investigators participating in a program. Another supportive document, the Investigator's Brochure, details information amassed at different stages throughout a drug's life cycle. Although less rhetorically inviting to the skilled medical writer, supportive materials nonetheless provide integral information for the drug's regulatory approval and therapeutic use.

PUBLICATION DOCUMENTS FOR THE MEDICAL COMMUNITY

Increasingly important in the evolving healthcare arena, publication documents digest information from regulatory documents to craft key messages for the external medical community. Besides being confidential in nature, regulatory documents target an audience requiring substantially more information than a practicing physician, nurse, or pharmacist. Reams of data from a clinical trial report, for example, need to be distilled into specific molds: manuscripts for scientific journals; abstracts, slides, and posters to be presented at professional conferences; and pithy copy for advertising purposes (Table 3.2). The following overview of these types of publication documents, typically handled by medical writers, supplements the details provided in Part III.

Manuscripts in scientific journals (Chapter 12) link the pharmaceutical researcher to the external medical community. Whether nonclinical or clinical, each research report contains valuable information on new or existing therapies, on methods of assessing pharmacological action, or on underlying mechanisms of health and disease. Medical writers cull information from the research report,

TABLE 3.2. Examples of Publication Documents

Type of publication document	Typical examples
Manuscripts for scientific journals	Article on a Phase IV clinical trial
	Review of a disease's treatments
Materials for professional meetings	Abstract of a trial's findings
	Poster on a new technique
Promotional pieces and advertising	Advertisement copy for a new drug
	Handouts for a sales force

fashioning journal manuscripts that provide key data, yet hook the reader's interest. Manuscripts weave these findings into the fabric of established scientific literature. Along with these commonalities, journal publishers establish format specifications and editorial policies to be followed.

Materials for professional meetings (Chapter 13) comprise a collection of output formats that further accentuate key messages from research trials. Scientists often rush to share their latest information on new therapies or methodological techniques. Because of lag times for publishing in journals, periodic conferences of professional societies (e.g., American Medical Association) facilitate the timely dissemination of important new findings—but at the tradeoff of even shorter presentational formats. An abstract of a research trial, for example, allows just one paragraph or page to summarize a full report! Similarly, one poster accommodates only a limited number of individual boards for text, tables, and graphics, let alone white space. And allotted speaking time confines the number of slides for any one presentation. Such format limitations thus challenge the medical writer's rhetorical skills and interpretive instincts.

Promotional pieces and advertising (Chapter 14) differ from other types of publication documents in that overall messages on a drug's therapeutic profile must be molded into short but balanced statements, complemented by visual graphics. Two or three lines of text, perhaps followed by a bulleted list, must accurately summarize a drug's profile, at least in terms of focal features (e.g., quality of life) for that advertising piece or sales brochure. Color, position, and wordplay accentuate the principal message; yet, promotional pieces must remain supported by the approved product labeling. Medical writers not only craft the text or other aspects of such pieces, but must also safeguard the ethical balance of presented information. Regulatory guidelines provide the key framework within which the medical writer operates for such documents.

RHETORICAL STRATEGIES FOR PHARMACEUTICAL DOCUMENTS

Pharmaceutical documents seek to record the findings of extensive research, but also to persuade the reader of its validity. Despite its inherent validity, however, a fact's acceptance as true remains influenced by the mode and style of its presentation (Lamm, 1994). Technical information particularly relies on firm rhetorical strategies for accurate transmission, requiring devices for easy access to and clear guidance through the otherwise maze of information (Orna, 1985). Remember: the writer's knows the destination, but the reader must find the path. Thus, the two categories of regulatory and publication documents challenge the medical writer to suit rhetorical strategy to target audience (Figure 3.1).

Although typically large and jammed with text information and tabular data, regulatory documents benefit from a captive audience. External users (e.g., FDA reviewers) must carefully review these documents as part of the drug approval process; and internal users (e.g., scientists) rely on this agreed record of a trial's findings as the foundation for additional research. Medical writers thus need to employ navigational devices, such as comprehensive tables of contents, and hierarchical numbering of sections. Additionally, readability requires clear and concise sentences to counterbalance the polysyllabic terms rampant in the medical sciences. Moreover, regulatory documents record findings in an unbiased manner; an overtly persuasive style would undermine a reviewer's comfort with the document's accuracy.

On the other hand, publication documents usually remain short because of limited space in scientific journals or for conference

FIGURE 3.1. Rhetorical Strategies and Target Audiences in Medical Writing

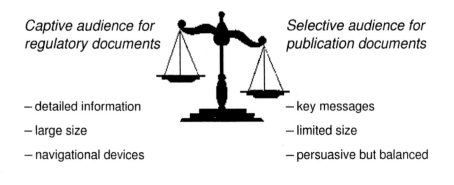

Captive audience for
regulatory documents

Selective audience for
publication documents

– detailed information

– large size

– navigational devices

– key messages

– limited size

– persuasive but balanced

materials. Hence, navigational guides play a smaller role. Still, medical writers must identify key messages and their most effective presentational format (e.g., text, table, or graph, but not all three). And the reader's attention must be hooked: Why should a selective audience read this article, rather than the others in that journal? Persuasive techniques that catch the reader's eye include titles beginning with a unique word, and white space that guides the eye to pivotal data displays. Striking the correct balance of information and presentation challenges medical writers—whether new to the craft, or seasoned over years.

These differences in rhetorical strategies, based on the main categories of regulatory and publication documents, illustrate the variety of challenges awaiting the medical writer in the field of drug development. The professional role of medical writers, their background and skills, and working interactions with other colleagues form the topic of the next chapter.

Chapter 4

Professional Roles of Medical Writers

If you want to set up your everlasting rest,
you are far more likely to find it in the life of the mind
than in the life of the heart.

—Dorothy L. Sayers

Whether handling regulatory or publication documents, the medical writer must bring a conglomeration of educational backgrounds, technical skills, and personal qualities for success. Diversity remains an understatement for such attributes (Chapter 1, "Basic Introduction to Medical Writing"). An overview of these typical characteristics follows.

STRUCTURE OF MEDICAL-WRITING GROUPS

Within the pharmaceutical industry, medical-writing groups provide key communication services that support the research and development of new drugs, and the continued safe and effective use of marketed products. This group's mission is to prepare high-quality documentation in support of company initiatives to develop new drugs that not only recoup on financial invest, but also contribute to health care. As detailed in Chapter 3 ("Types of Pharmaceutical Documents"), the services of medical-writing groups encompass regulatory documents that focus on government approval, and publication documents that target the external medical community.

In providing this wide scope of document services, medical-writing groups comprise a variety of personnel functions. Obviously, medical writers themselves form the basis of any medical-writing group; but medical writers may individually specialize in one of these two document types in larger groups, or may cover both types in smaller ones. Depending on the company structure, regulatory and publication groups may indeed be separate corporate entities, sometimes in separate departments (e.g., research and marketing, respectively). In larger groups, medical writers may form distinct teams, each specializing in certain therapeutic areas.

Additionally, peripheral personnel integrally support the important work of medical-writing groups. Such support services often depend on the overall structure of the company itself; for example, computer services may be provided from a centralized group across entire departments, or this responsibility may reside with individuals within a medical-writing group. This situation is analogous to that of separate or combined groups for regulatory and publication documents: a matter of organizational structure, not inherent philosophy.

Irrespective of corporate philosophy, the following support services remain pivotal to the success of medical-writing endeavors:

- *Technical editing*—to maintain consistent house style and language standards
- *Quality control*—to ensure the integrity of all documentation
- *Electronic publishing*—to facilitate document production and dissemination
- *Document management*—to control intermediate and archival versions
- *Administrative support*—to handle budgets and related bureaucracies

Other important services (which may be combined in the above categories) include secretarial support, final proofreading, developmental training, process improvement, and supervisory management. Figure 4.1 illustrates the organizational structure of a representative medical-writing group.

BACKGROUND, SKILLS, AND EDUCATION

Regardless of group structure, certain qualities describe a "typical" medical writer. By the nature of their work, medical writers must balance between technical skills in the medical sciences and rhetorical skills in the language arts. Finding the optimal balance requires a shift from pure science, since medical writing focuses on

FIGURE 4.1. Representative Organization of a Medical-Writing Group

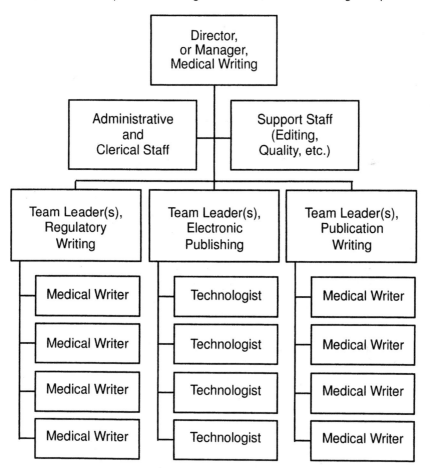

expression—not the explicit development—of scientific knowledge (Losi, 1987a).

This balance between science and language is reflected in results from a 1986 survey of the American Medical Writers Association (AMWA) (Losi, 1987b), a major professional group for medical writers. For highest educational level, respondents were closely split between those with a graduate or professional degree (50.6 percent) versus those with an undergraduate degree (45.5 percent); few

(5.5 percent) lacked a formal degree. Almost half (46.2 percent) indicated science as their primary educational background; slightly less (37.6 percent) indicated humanities or journalism (Table 4.1). Relevant science areas include biology and other life sciences; pharmacology and other pharmaceutical areas; and medicine, nursing, and the various healthcare fields.

Additional opportunities beyond formal degrees, however, do exist for those interested in pursuing the medical-writing profession. Historically, those off-balance for the two skill areas have stronger science backgrounds, but a keen interest and proclivity for writing and communication. Such individuals may increase language skills through college courses, often in a continuing-education setting, while employed as a scientist. AMWA itself offers a certificate program that introduces medical writers to the basics of their field, along with specializations in subject areas, such as editing, freelancing, pharmaceutical, public relations, and audiovisual (AMWA, 1996).

TABLE 4.1. Educational Backgrounds of Medical Writers

Educational characteristic	Response (N = 1,321[a])	
	Number	Percent of total
Highest educational level:		
Graduate or professional degree	663	50.6
Undergraduate degree	596	45.5
No formal degree	50	3.9
Primary educational field:		
Science	604	46.2
Humanities or journalism	490	37.6
Other (e.g., social science, business)	212	16.2

Note: Data were adapted from Losi, 1987b.
[a] Total response equaled 1,321 of 2,600 members, but percentages were based on the number of usable responses per question (slightly less).

For medical writers "in-the-making," an academic program that combines science and language through two majors, a major and a minor, or two separate degrees would be the best advice. Moreover, colleges and universities are increasingly cognizant of the growing need for skilled medical writers, and of the opportunities for such educational programs. Often, these programs offer a general curriculum in technical writing, but with specializations or electives available in the medical field. In 1985, the Society for Technical Communications (another fine professional organization for technical writers) compiled a list of fifty-six institutions with academic programs in technical communication: six with Associate's degrees; thirty-seven with Bachelor's degrees; eighteen with Master's degrees; and sixteen with certificates (Kelley et al., 1985). Certainly, other programs will develop in time.

As a complication, however, the proper balance of science and language depends on the type of specialization sought by the medical writer (Figure 4.2). Those specializing in regulatory documents benefit from a stronger scientific base, since they contribute to the

FIGURE 4.2. Balance of Science and Language Skills in Medical Writing

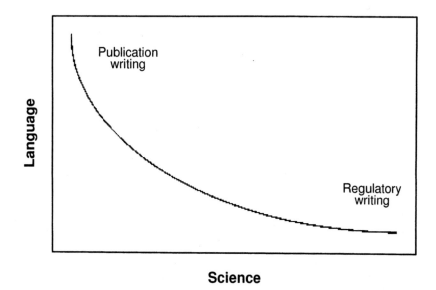

Publication writing

Regulatory writing

Language

Science

design and interpretation of trials. At the other end of the spectrum stand those specializing in publication documents, who require more rhetorical finesse for crafting documents that hook the interest of external healthcare professionals. But because medical writers may prepare both document types—or may even switch from one to the other during their careers—a moderate mix of both skill types remains optimal for effective contributions to the development of pharmaceutical documents.

TEAM APPROACH TO MEDICAL WRITING

In the profession of medical writing, knowledge and experience in the complementary areas of science and language provide the basic potential for success. Other qualities of the individual, however, also contribute. Foremost, potential medical writers must be sufficiently mature and self-supporting to thrive when working alone.

But the medical writers of today, even those who work on a freelance or contractor basis, spend increasingly larger proportions of their time within project teams. The medical writer would not necessarily be the medical or statistical expert, for example, but rather the language expert. Thus, project teams typically involve a core team who collaborate from the inception of a trial's protocol through its final report, and from the individual report through a drug's regulatory submission. Team members—usually a physician, clinical trial specialist, biostatistician, data programmer, and medical writer—shift lead roles throughout the project's life cycle, with the medical writer leading the team during stages of document production (Figure 4.3).

Thus, the medical writer plays a dual role in pharmaceutical research:

1. Individual contributor on specific writing projects
2. Team collaborator in program planning and development

Furthermore, the medical writer acts on two tiers of team involvement (Pakes, 1994):

1. Internal team of the medical-writing group
2. External team with other functional representatives

FIGURE 4.3. Relative Roles of Team Members During a Clinical Trial

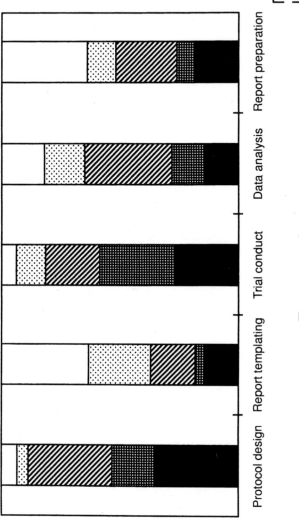

Relative effort

Protocol design Report templating Trial conduct Data analysis Report preparation

Team member

☐ Medical writer
▨ Programmer
▨ Biostatistician
▦ Trial specialist
■ Physician

The successful medical writer must therefore cultivate strong interpersonal skills for such internal and external team involvement. To illustrate this interplay of individual contributor and team collaborator, consider the following sequence representative of a document's life cycle:

1. Template of the document (medical writer; input of internal and external teams)
2. Preparation of first draft (medical writer; input of external team)
3. Review by project team (external team)
4. Revision to second draft (medical writer; input of internal team, such as editor)
5. Review by senior management (external team and their management)
6. Completion of final document (medical writer; also electronic publishing)
7. Approval of final document (management of project team)
8. Filing of paper and electronic renditions (medical writer and internal team)

As can be clearly seen, medical writers not only balance their academic skill areas, but also their time working individually and collaboratively. These interactions expand to capitalize on modern communication technology. Chapter 1 ("Basic Introduction to Medical Writing") hinted at this pivotal concept; Chapter 5 ("Publishing and Information Technology") expands on the role of technology in medical writing.

Chapter 5

Publishing and Information Technology

Art is a human activity having for its purpose
the transmission to others of the highest and best feelings
to which men have risen.

—Leo Tolstoy

Information technology both pulls and chases the field of medical writing. Not only do new computerized systems challenge the medical writer to capitalize on such amazing technologies, but the writer's need for sophisticated support structures itself drives the development of further technological advances. Moreover, though in the background, modern scientific breakthroughs, particularly for communications, preclude any medical writer from simply standing still!

This chapter discusses the ongoing effects of electronic publishing, computer graphics, and related technology on the practice of medical writing in pharmaceutical research—both now and in the future.

ELECTRONIC PUBLISHING
OF REGULATORY DOCUMENTS

Although complementary to publication documents for the external medical community, regulatory documents for drug submissions—in sheer bulk alone—weigh in at well over half of all pharmaceutical documents. The drive to remain evermore competitive forces pharmaceutical companies to shave time, but not quality, from every aspect of drug research. Regulatory documents stand square on the firing line: with every day saved in bringing a new drug to market equating up to one million dollars, the drug's regulatory documents are prime targets for cutting overall production time (Hoffman, 1996).

Computerized technologies to assist pharmaceutical companies and drug scientists in processing, storing, retrieving, and using the multitudinous piles of textual, tabular, and graphical components of traditional documents grow in complexity. A basic approach to managing such documents and subdocuments stems from optical imaging. Think of laser disks for music, but substitute image visualizations of reports instead. Optical imaging compresses paper documents onto laser platters "played on jukeboxes," with data bases supporting quick searching capabilities at the user's desktop. Though not a substitute for true electronic publishing, optical imaging allows companies to manage information in a more secure and relatively quick manner. Optical imaging provides its own benefits, especially for those documents not easily available in electronic format (Alwitt and Kinney, 1993).

But electronic publishing strides boldly beyond optical imaging. Building on desktop systems commonly available today, true electronic publishing utilizes complex filters to convert documents from diverse sources (e.g., wordprocessing text, spreadsheet or statistical tables, computer graphics, and optical images) into one coherent structure (Figure 5.1). Imagine the immediate benefits of one system containing all components of a complex document typical for a drug submission. And the future benefits . . .

FIGURE 5.1. Input Sources for Electronic Publishing of Regulatory Submissions

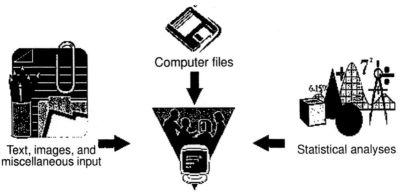

Computer files

Text, images, and miscellaneous input

Statistical analyses

Electronic-publishing system

Yet, do not discount the cost. Medical writers now must rely on strong technological staff for support in the electronic publishing of their increasingly complex documents (see Chapter 4, "Professional Roles of Medical Writers"). Quicker information flow may use fewer medical writers, but with total headcount balanced—or perhaps increased—by additional computer staff. Furthermore, myriad systems for electronic publishing introduce countless permutations of hardware, software, and standards for creating documents (Studebaker, 1993).

For example, Company X may prefer software 1, hardware 2, and standard 3 for many good reasons; but, if Company Y prefers a different set, then how will the US FDA or other regulatory agencies deal with this complexity? Differences like these can occur across departments within the same company, further complicating this juggernaut of information technology. For good reasons, many companies now deliberately select common standards, such as SGML (Standard Generalized Markup Language), for the basic structure for all published documents.

Among the international agencies that govern the marketing of drugs, the FDA stands at the forefront in requiring pharmaceutical companies to capitalize on technology to speed the approval process. For the US, a regulatory submission no longer remains "just" a paper New Drug Application or NDA, but now must also be transformed into the complementary form of a *Computer-Assisted* New Drug Application or *CA*NDA (Accomando, 1993). Although beyond the scope of this chapter, suffice it to say that customized systems for electronic publishing facilitate preparation of such computer-assisted filings (Smith, Naughton, and Bonk, 1995).

COMPUTERIZED SUPPORT FOR PUBLICATION DOCUMENTS

In addition to regulatory submissions, publication documents also benefit from direct applications of information technology. Rather than managing bulk size and complex formats for regulatory submissions, challenges for publication documents focus on disseminating effective information to a complex external audience (see Chapter 3, "Types of Pharmaceutical Documents").

The issues inherent in the electronic publishing of regulatory submissions apply to the creation of publication documents, albeit in a less complex manner due to differences in size alone. Regardless, publishing houses increasingly use these computerized systems to receive, classify, assemble, edit, and print manuscripts and other related documents. In the competitive environment of publishing, no medical writer can afford to lose time or opportunity for lack of optimal computer support. Fortunately for these medical writers, publications must meet the standards of the external recipient at the publishing house, thereby circumventing internal convolutions for drug submissions.

As electronic publishing matures in leaps and bounds, new tools assist the medical writer and technological staff in quickly producing effective publications. Software now allows not just creation of document components such as text, tables, and graphs, but furthermore supports automated techniques for page layout and overall design of high-quality documents, often with reduced costs and time (Wasserman, 1990). Computer systems also allow more effective processes for indexing, storing, and retrieving both internal and external documents for subsequent publication (Warr, 1991). In essence, the computerized production of publication documents forms a sleek conduit between authors and publishers not possible without information technology (Figure 5.2).

FUTURE IMPLICATIONS OF INFORMATION TECHNOLOGY

Overall, new information technologies propel medical writers into an exciting future of professional growth and personal challenge: professional growth from edged nuances in the role of medical writing; personal challenge from honed techniques and creative applications. In fact, the cognitive skills for processing and applying such abundance of information from information technology forms our future (Lunin, 1981).

Pessimists may worry that sophisticated computerization makes obsolete the medical writer of yesterday; but we optimists know that this explosion of healthcare information swings wide the door for the medical writer of tomorrow.

FIGURE 5.2. Information Technology as a Conduit for External Publications

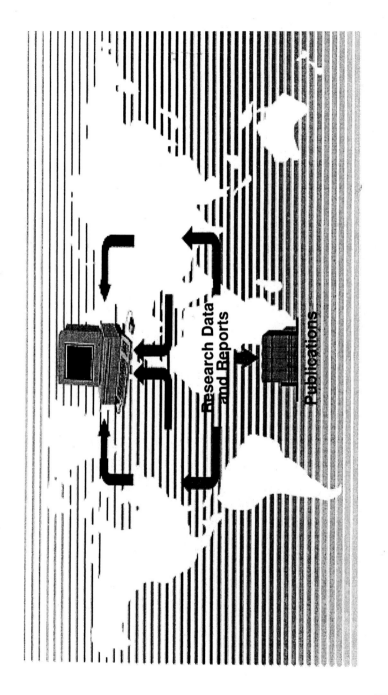

PART II:
REGULATORY DOCUMENTS
FOR DRUG SUBMISSIONS

As one of two main categories of pharmaceutical documents, regulatory submissions form a mainstay of medical writing within drug research. Part II develops the structural constraints and rhetorical approaches for regulatory documents.

Chapter 6

Structure of Regulatory Submissions

Prose is architecture, not interior decoration,
and the Baroque is over.

—Ernest Hemingway

Regulatory submissions represent the culmination of a decade's research on each new drug. Obviously, such a complex process requires professional input from many technical specialists, ranging from bench scientists who design each new drug, to clinical physicians who monitor its testing in human trials. Presenting this detailed information in scientifically unbiased, yet technically convincing, language forms the crux of the medical writer's role in drug submissions, as detailed in this chapter.

PYRAMIDAL STRUCTURE
OF REGULATORY SUBMISSIONS

Because a regulatory submission synthesizes information amassed during a decade from various technical sources, this compendium of documents is voluminous. In fact, "voluminous" is the technically correct term: agency standards dictate division of these regulatory submissions, such as an NDA (New Drug Application) in the United States, into "volumes" of certain length, in a particular order, with color-coded covers, divided into tabbed subsections!

But stand back for a moment from this overwhelming pile of information and gain the proper perspective on the overall structure of a regulatory submission (e.g., NDA). The structure of this compendium generally assumes the form of a pyramid (Figure 6.1). The pinnacle of this pyramid represents the highest-level summary of

FIGURE 6.1. Pyramidal Structure of a Regulatory Submission

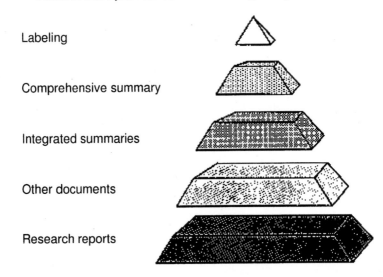

Labeling

Comprehensive summary

Integrated summaries

Other documents

Research reports

information—the drug label or package insert that patients may often read in these days of consumer awareness. Underpinning this distillation of key information are other summaries, such as toxicology, pharmacokinetics, efficacy, safety, or other associated categories of information. Eventually, one drills down to individual reports, the basic building blocks holding the entire pyramid intact. As the document hierarchy reaches upward to the pinnacle of the label, the overall strength of the pyramidal submission depends on this firm foundation of individual reports.

The regulatory submission itself, though, can be viewed as a linking set of pyramids. For example, the clinical information builds from clinical trial reports (as detailed in Chapter 7, "Foundation Reports of Research Trials"), through integrated summaries of efficacy and safety, finally reaching its own subpinnacle of a clinical data summary (see Chapter 8, "Overview and Summary Documents").

Using the NDA as a prototype, the regulatory submission comprises a defined set of thirteen "items," or major subdivisions (Table 6.1). These items divide the submission into units that can be individually sent for review by specialist reviewers at the agency. As a case

TABLE 6.1. Submission Structure Exemplified by NDA Items

Item	Title
1	Table of Contents
2	Comprehensive Summary
3	Chemistry, Manufacturing, and Controls System
4	Samples, Methods Validation, and Labeling Package
5	Nonclinical Pharmacology and Toxicology Section
6	Human Pharmacokinetics and Bioavailability Section
7	Microbiology Section (if the drug is an antibiotic)
8	Clinical Data Section
9	Safety Update Report
10	Statistical Section
11	Case Report Tabulations
12	Case Report Forms
13	Patent Information

NDA = New Drug Application

in point, all reviewers would receive Item 2, Comprehensive Summary, to get a full view of the drug's profile; but the nonclinical pharmacologist would receive Item 5, Nonclinical Pharmacology and Toxicology Section, whereas the clinical reviewer would receive Item 8, Clinical Data Section. In an NDA, each item has its own guideline about preparation, structure, and content, such as for Item 8 (U.S. Department of Health and Human Services, 1988).

Within each item, a pyramidal hierarchy also provides the basic structure that allows the agency reviewer to navigate through the amassed information. Tables 6.2 and 6.3 provide the major breakdown of Items 2 and 8, respectively, as examples to indicate the particular subdocuments typically involving key work from a medical writer. Other documents may be written by a scientist instead, perhaps with an editorial review by a medical writer as an internal mechanism for overall consistency.

TABLE 6.2. Subdivision Structure of NDA Item 2, Comprehensive Summary

Section	Title
A	Proposed Text of the Labeling for the Drug—Annotated
B	Pharmaceutical Class, Scientific Rationale, Intended Use, and Potential Clinical Benefits[a]
C	Foreign Marketing History
D	Chemistry, Manufacturing, and Controls Summary
E	Nonclinical Pharmacology and Toxicology Summary
F	Human Pharmacokinetics and Bioavailability Summary
G	Microbiology Summary (if the drug is an antibiotic)
H	Clinical Data Summary and Results of Statistical Analysis[a]
I	Discussion of Benefit/Risk Relationship and Proposed Post-marketing Studies[a]

[a]Typically involves the medical writer in a key role.
NDA = New Drug Application

TABLE 6.3. Subdivision Structure of NDA Item 8, Clinical Data Section

Section	Title
A	Index, List of Investigators, and List of INDs and NDAs
B	Background and Overview of Clinical Investigations[a]
C	Clinical Pharmacology (tabular summary and report synopses)[a]
D	Controlled Clinical Trials (tabular summary and full reports)[a]
E	Uncontrolled Clinical Trials (tabular summary and full reports)[a]
F	Other Studies and Information (tabular summary and full reports)[a]
G	Integrated Summary of Effectiveness Data[a]
H	Integrated Summary of Safety Information[a]
I	Drug Abuse and Overdose Information
J	Integrated Summary of Benefits and Risks of the Drug[a]

[a]Typically involves the medical writer in a key role.
IND = Investigational New Drug
NDA = New Drug Application

Although this book's size precludes detailed discussion of each subsection of an NDA, other chapters within Part II, "Regulatory Documents for Drug Submissions," provide an overview of this pyramidal structure. Consult other agency guidelines, as well as the Food and Drug Law itself (Food and Drug Law Institute, 1995) for additional specifics about a particular item, section, or requirement.

TEAM INTERACTIONS FOR THE MEDICAL WRITER

Each regulatory submission requires the dedicated input of a team of professionals, each bringing their expertise to the project. Such members include (but are not limited to) toxicologists, pharmacologists, pharmacokineticists, physicians, statisticians, and medical writers. Each member must work with the others toward their common and ultimate goal—production of a scientifically sound and user-friendly compendium that documents the drug's profile (Mannion et al., 1994). Strategic and operational planning throughout this complex process strongly contributes to the successful achievement of this goal.

Consider, for example, the development of any new drug. The clinical section alone (Item 8) may comprise ten to fifty individual trials, each with its own report that must be segregated into the appropriate subsection (e.g., 8C, 8D, 8E, or 8F). Each report will involve many interactions from its own project team, from startup to completion of the actual trial, through coding and analysis of the data, and then writing and revising the final report (see Chapter 7, "Foundation Reports of Research Trials," for details).

Keeping each report on track requires an agreed and followed time table for the entire project team; time tables for the higher-level documents in the submission pyramid similarly derive from these report time tables. Just as the information in the higher-level summaries and pinnacle documents rely on firm footing on the foundation reports, the time table for completing the overall submission likewise stands on time tables for each individual report. In this interlinking structure, the medical writer becomes a key player, who is responsible for the final, and thus more visible, stage of report production. The medical writer must effectively interact with all project members and contributors so that the report, summary, or other document proceeds as closely to schedule as possible.

Moreover, the medical writer must diligently work to ensure that the document's quality remains high because a timely, but unusable, document does not contribute to an effective regulatory submission. The consistency, readability, format, and presentation of the document depends on rhetorical skills of the medical writer. Indeed, readability becomes key in these documents filled with polysyllabic terms. The finesse of the medical writer assumes even greater importance in higher-level summaries, given that such documents must summarize a drug's profile in a more limited space. Specific documents for European submissions (e.g., Expert Reports) provide additional challenges because of their more interpretive approach.

With rhetorical strategy as the cement for the building blocks, regulatory guidelines provide the basic blueprint from which the medical writer and project team construct a technically firm and easily navigable document that ultimately leads to an effective submission package for the new drug candidate. Approaches for specific document types form the basis of the following four chapters.

Chapter 7

Foundation Reports of Research Trials

I am an obsessive writer, doing one draft and then another
and another, usually five.
In a way I have nothing to say, but a great deal to add.

—Gore Vidal

Forming the basis of the pyramidal structure of regulatory submissions, foundation reports summarize scientific findings from research trials. Each trial requires a formal report to document its methods, results, and interpretation. This research report becomes a vehicle for compiling the information, determining its meaning, assessing its implications, documenting the findings, and especially communicating the outcomes.

Clinical trial reports exemplify the basic structure and rhetorical approach for such documents. This chapter explains the rhetorical strategy and main sections of a clinical trial report, contrasting these elements with those of other document types. Appended is an instructional template customizable to the specific needs of a drug program, therapeutic area, or corporate strategy.

GUIDELINES FOR RESEARCH REPORTS

Because research reports represent the formal documentation of clinical or other trials conducted for the development of a drug, specific guidelines determine their content, format, and medium (e.g., paper hard copy versus electronic file). Complicating this further, guidelines can vary according to the type of research trial (e.g., nonclinical in animals versus clinical in humans), therapeutic category of the drug (e.g., antibiotics involve additional microbiological testing), and even the country in which the drug is to be marketed. Additionally, each drug company may design its own nuances so that its reports are recognizable to health regulatory agencies.

Fortunately, countries and companies realize that efficient development of new drugs and dissemination of research findings require streamlined processes and formats for reports. The European Community, for example, continues to blend requirements for research reports on drugs so that one standard report should apply to all agreeing countries. Of paramount importance to this standardization of research reports is ongoing work by the International Conference on Harmonization (Nightingale, 1995). Representing drug regulatory agencies from major countries worldwide, this group has proferred one set of guidelines to dictate the acceptable structure of a research report. Although guidelines remain subject to interpretation, this key effort bodes well for more efficient and less frustrating efforts by medical writers in drug development.

CLINICAL TRIAL REPORT AS AN EXAMPLE

All research reports share a common backbone comprising four sections: introduction, methods, results, and conclusions. The details contained within this structure depend, however, on the underlying nature of its trial. For example, nonclinical trials in animals would contain certain subcategories, such as toxicological findings, that would not be in clinical reports in humans; and vice versa. For example, the general format of a clinical trial report can be used, since clinical research in humans often occupies the bulk of effort by medical writers in drug development.

In any scientific discipline, research reports lay the foundation for more comprehensive compilations of information. Each report documents the findings of its research trial; without this lower-level documentation, similarities and differences across trials could not be determined at a higher vantage. Melding information into further hypotheses and theories would be precluded.

Drug development also depends on a firm base of research reports to produce the overall regulatory submission, or New Drug Application (NDA), as it is termed in the United States. Integrated summaries that overview the efficacy and safety profiles of a new drug, for example, rely on those types of information as documented in each of the individual reports. From this foundation of research reports as building blocks, the pyramidal structure ultimately leading to various integrated summaries, and finally the product labeling itself, can be generated (as detailed in Chapter 6, "Structure of Regulatory Submissions").

Appendix A details a typical format for a clinical trial report. Instructions on its substantive content and rhetorical presentation complement the numbered headings and subheadings. This format generally follows the structure outlined by the United States Food and Drug Administration (FDA) in recent guidelines (U.S. Food and Drug Administration, 1988). But because these guidelines must mesh with results of the International Conference on Harmonization, as well as for individual corporate strategies, the supplied format should be considered an example or model, not a definitive dictum.

Remember: always verify the report structure required for each particular situation. This includes checking the latest guidelines from regulatory agencies, such as the FDA, along with specific nuances of each drug program.

RHETORICAL STRATEGY OF RESEARCH REPORTS

A research report, such as a clinical trial report, documents the purpose, techniques, findings, and meanings of the trial. The key point of communication for the investigator, trial sponsor, and medical writer is to critically present the findings in sufficient detail for others to evaluate the trial's outcome (Friedman, Furberg, and DeMets, 1984).

Rhetorically, then, a research report is factual, scientific, and detailed. But this very nature of detail for a report mandates that clear and concise wording be utilized in an unambiguous and straightforward manner. Medical terminology in particular is fraught with convoluted conventions for polysyllabic names; drugs, too, suffer from difficult wording, even in the simple case of aspirin, or, more specifically, acetylsalicylic acid. Or consider all of the details from a patient's hospital chart that might need inclusion in narrative description of an adverse event reported by the patient while enrolled in the research trial, particularly a trial in a therapeutic area such as cancer that requires trials extending over several years.

Hence, for research reports, use basic techniques of technical writing:

1. Keep the sentence structure simple.
2. Identify hierarchy through a section-numbering convention.
3. Steer navigation with a table of contents.
4. Tabulate data to support text statements.
5. Graphically portray trends to be gleaned from the results.
6. Cross-refer to other sections for related information.
7. Append supportive documentation outside the main report body.

Guidelines for reports often list such logical precepts as these. Yet, for emphasis, the repetition here leaves no room for excuses!

COMPARISONS WITH RELATED DOCUMENTS

As foundation documents, research reports provide the groundwork for other key documents. Particularly, reports are used to generate higher-level NDA summaries (see Chapter 8, "Overview and Summary Documents") and journal manuscripts (see Chapter 12, "Manuscripts in Scientific Journals"). Through comparison with these other document types, the underlying structure and rhetorical intent of a clinical trial report can be more fully understood.

Table 7.1 lists distinguishing differences between clinical trial reports and higher-level summaries, such as those for efficacy or safety information across the entire drug program. Because a summary distills key information from many reports, it remains less detailed, particularly for administrative or supportive issues. A report focuses on results for the trial's specific objectives, whereas a higher-level summary seeks an overall interpretation of related results. While a report comprises results from various types of assessments and procedures, a higher-level summary groups only those findings related to that document's intent (e.g., efficacy versus safety, but not both).

Comparison of a research report with a journal publication (Table 7.2) uncovers a different set of distinguishing features. Although a report and manuscript both document findings of one trial, their

TABLE 7.1. Comparison of a Research Report and a Higher-Level Summary

Research report	Higher-level summary
Details findings of one individual trial	Integrates findings across trial groups
Provides details of administrative items	Cross-refers to other document details
Focuses on results versus objectives	Focuses on overall interpretation
Includes results for all assessments	Groups findings by document intent
(e.g., efficacy *and* safety)	(e.g., efficacy *versus* safety)

TABLE 7.2. Comparison of a Research Report and a Journal Manuscript

Research report	Journal manuscript
Targets reviewer at regulatory agency	Captures provider in medical community
Provides results for all assessments	Highlights main results of interest
Minimizes use of literature reviews	Compares results with literature
Grows in overall size (1,000s of pages)	Limits final printed size (5 to 15 pages)
Uses table of contents for navigation	Prescribes format for heading structure

audiences require decidedly antipodal strategies: a report targets a captive regulatory reviewer, whereas a manuscript competes for the attention of busy healthcare professionals. The levels of detail also differ, since a report documents all methods and results, whereas a manuscript highlights those key to the journal's readers. Given these levels of detail, a report's final size dwarfs that of a manuscript, with its limited journal pages. The report's larger size correspondingly requires more navigational tools, such as a table of contents and numbered section headings; a journal's editorial style dictates the format allowed for such document techniques. Finally, wider interpretation of results, in the context of other scientific literature, usually remains outside the scope of the report itself, but fully appropriate for the discussion section required in a typical manuscript.

As can be seen in this comparison with the NDA summary or journal manuscript, the foundation report logically precedes these derived document types. Pressures to bring drugs to market sooner and sooner, however, often collapse time frames such that these activities begin to overlap. When this occurs, the medical writer must ensure that any updated information reaches all relevant documents for consistency. Sophisticated technology (as discussed in Chapter 5, "Publishing and Information Technology") facilitates these updates. Still, a final proofreading check is always advisable.

Chapter 8

Overview and Summary Documents

After all, one knows one's weak points so well, that it's rather bewildering to have the critics overlook them & invent others.

—Edith Wharton

With research reports as the foundation, regulatory submissions weave a hierarchy of comprehensive overview and summary documents. These summaries of efficacy, safety, and other assessment criteria weave complex facts into a coherent message. Although the substantive content varies across documents according to the discipline represented (e.g., nonclinical toxicology versus clinical safety), all overview and summary documents share a common goal: highlighting key points from many reports to deliver a key message to the regulatory reviewer.

In this chapter, common approaches that medical writers take in building these pivotal documents are examined. A selected template provides a working model for building any of these overview or summary documents.

OVERALL GOALS OF DOCUMENT INTEGRATION

For the moment, let's forget about specific scientific disciplines, such as toxicology. Instead, concentrate on the overall goals of integrating key information from reports into overview and summary documents to be analyzed by regulatory agencies who determine whether to approve a new drug for marketing in its therapeutic indication. What would be the overall goals, then, of such higher-level documents?

First, the writer must provide the information specified by agency guidelines for any particular document. FDA guidelines, for example, dictate the issues to be addressed or considered for the various subdocuments in Item 2, the Comprehensive Summary, or in Item 8, the Clinical Data Section (U.S. Department of Health and Human Services, 1987 and 1988, respectively). In some cases, such guidelines detail exact points that must be covered for the regulatory submission to be filed with the agency. In other cases, the guidelines may provide discussion to consider in tailoring the document for the specific drug and therapeutic indication. An excellent case in point is the Integrated Summary of Benefits and Risks of the Drug, a short document (five to ten pages) that weighs the drug's potential benefits against its known risks. The FDA requires that this integrated summary briefly compare key evidence of effectiveness with main adverse events. More detailed discussions may be appropriate for special situations, such as a limited data base for a drug that targets a rare disease. Considering patient versus societal perspectives can also be relevant for such analyses (Spilker, 1991).

Second, the writer must understand the full interrelationships of these overview and summary documents within the pyramidal structure of a regulatory submission. Recall from Chapter 6, "Structure of Regulatory Submissions," that a submission tapers from a broad foundation of research reports, through focusing levels of integrated documents, ultimately reaching the pinnacle of the drug label (see Figure 6.1). To sculpt the focus of these documents, the writer must maintain proper perspective on each document's topic: toxicology, efficacy, safety, or similar categories. Reports may be represented according to their importance to the overall program, as well as the relevance and substantiability of their findings. Effecting this perspective depends on the writer's involvement with the program throughout its development; use of "extra hands" during rush periods before filing the submission may only dilute the consistent efforts that skilled medical writers contribute.

Third and ultimately, the writer must ensure that the document's message stems from an unbiased presentation of evidence in fact. Enthusiasm of scientists so close to the drug's development may engender conclusions that, while based on data, may not be evident to a third-party reader without substantiation. Key benefits of the drug, in terms of efficacy for the intended indication, must be viewed through a prism revealing the therapeutic aspects important to wider use in the general population. Similarly, the potential for adverse events and other side effects must be scrutinized as carefully as possible, as a safeguard before marketing can be approved.

By working closely as a core member of the project team, the medical writer can bring a leveling eye across masses of data. Certainly, the writer should not profess to be a clinician or biostatistician (unless also meeting the unique sets of skills and credentials for these specialty areas). Through close interactions with such specialists, however, the writer can often bring seemingly disparate sources of information into focus for overview and summary documents that deliver the intended messages about the drug's investigational program.

RHETORICAL APPROACHES FOR SUMMARY DOCUMENTS

Successfully meeting these three objectives for overview and summary documents requires selection of effective rhetorical approaches. Typical strategies, as listed in Table 8.1, illustrate techniques that the writer can employ in crafting sound documents that integrate information across a drug program.

First, fulfilling the agency requirements assumes that the writer not only understands relevant guidelines, but can interpret them operationally for the drug being assessed. The writer must address each required element in a checklist approach, ensuring that each is addressed (or explained if not relevant). Additionally, the writer

TABLE 8.1. Rhetorical Strategies for Regulatory Overview Documents

Underlying objective	Rhetorical approach
Fulfill agency requirements	Systematically delineate required elements
Achieve hierarchical placement	View document as a related piece of many
Substantiate key messages	Detail evidence in a logical sequence

must also interpret the application of suggested or optional criteria because many depend on the drug and its therapeutic indication. Item 7, Microbiology Section, for example, is only appropriate if the drug is an antibiotic. Others are not as obvious.

Second, achieving the hierarchical placement of an overview document requires the writer to understand the complex relationships across document types. The Integrated Summary of Effectiveness Data (Section 8G) and the Integrated Summary of Safety Information (Section 8H) each present highlights of efficacy and safety, respectively, across all clinical trials. But the Integrated Summary of Benefits and Risks of the Drug (Section 8J) weighs potential benefits and known risks to the patient. Each underlying document should thus be written in view of the key points that higher-level documents will need to glean from mounds of data; this process should be smoothly built into the document strategies themselves.

Third, substantiating key messages in an unbiased fashion mandates that the writer build layer upon layer of evidence to support conclusions within the document. It does not matter if the scientists reached these conclusions inductively, deductively, or in a hybrid fashion; the writer must clearly present the conclusion, and then logically detail the data findings that build this case. Interestingly, substantiation of these key messages involves aspects of the previous two rhetorical approaches: applying sound knowledge of relevant guidelines; and viewing each document as a piece of the whole. Indeed, the writer's rhetorical strategies mirror the pyramidal structure of the regulatory submission itself.

TYPICAL EXAMPLES AS DOCUMENT MODELS

Regulatory guidelines compartmentalize submissions into a selection of overview and summary documents, usually by scientific discipline (e.g., toxicology or pharmacology). Each of the nine sections of the Comprehensive Summary (Item 2, Sections 2A to 2I), for example, generally represents a separate summarization of key information (see Chapter 6, Table 6.2). Appendix B provides a working template for Section 2H, Clinical Data Summary and Results of Statistical Analysis, as a document model. This overview document summarizes information from all individual trials in the clinical program, segregating them by category (e.g., controlled versus uncontrolled trials), and integrating certain data types (e.g., safety). Other overview and summary documents could be comparably modeled.

Supporting these overview and summary documents, though, are not just foundation reports, but also shorter pieces perhaps more administrative or limited in scope. The next chapter explores such supportive materials for regulatory submissions.

Chapter 9

Supportive Materials for Submissions

I had the need to note or preserve every fugitive image, and to struggle against the impermanence of both things and myself.

—Pierre Loti

Research reports and summary documents form the building blocks of regulatory submissions. But as for any building able to withstand the elements, strong mortar must cement the pieces together: supportive or administrative documents provide this mortar. Though perhaps lacking the rhetorical elan of more complex documents, these documents comprise a wide variety of types to meet their specific purposes: some may be short pieces of text; others, tables often continuing for many pages; and the rest, such as the Investigator's Brochure, amalgams of these two types.

This chapter reviews representative documents supporting regulatory submissions. Examples of typical information illustrate the construction of document templates for such supportive materials.

NARRATIVE DOCUMENTS FOR ADMINISTRATIVE SUPPORT

In regulatory submissions, certain documents that comprise mainly text administratively support the overall package. Although each NDA section (see Chapter 6, "Structure of Regulatory Submissions") maintains its own focus (e.g., nonclinical versus clinical), all share certain administrative needs. Sections in Item 2, Comprehensive Summary, provide basic information for all regulatory reviewers, whereas those in Item 8, Clinical Data Section, for example, target administrative needs of that area (U.S. Department of

Health and Human Services, 1987). Examples of both types of supportive narrative documents follow.

Section 2B, Pharmacologic Class, Scientific Rationale, and Potential Clinical Benefits, targets all regulatory reviewers. This documents delivers exactly what its title purports:

1. Definition of the pharmacologic class of the drug moiety under study
2. Justification for the scientific rationale underpinning the research program
3. Delineation of the clinical benefits expected from the drug's proposed use

Generally, Section 2B should be brief (perhaps ten to fifteen pages), organized, and pithy. Remember that Item 2 must fit within one submission volume, or roughly 300 pages. With Section 2H, Clinical Data Summary and Results of Statistical Analysis, comprising about half (see Chapter 8), other supportive sections must be concise.

In contrast to Section 2B, which targets all regulatory reviewers, Section 8B, Background/Overview of Clinical Investigations, primarily focuses on clinical reviewers. Section 8B describes the scientific setting in which the clinical program for the new drug was developed. This narrative document addresses the following key points:

- Rationale for critical design features of trials (e.g., dosing, controls, end points)
- Relationship of clinical pharmacology findings to critical features of trial design
- References to regulatory guidelines used, with explanations for any deviations
- Summarization of key decisions from discussions between sponsor and agency
- Selection of demographic subgroups (e.g., pediatric versus elderly) for study
- Potential issues of efficacy or safety experienced with similar therapeutic agents
- Areas for further research, including any clinical trials pending or in progress

In essence, Section 8B summarizes the science behind the clinical program, as needed for the clinical reviewers, whereas Section 2B summarizes the science behind the drug itself, as needed for the wider scope of all submission reviewers. Other items of the NDA may also include similar administrative documents whose text sets the scene for the information included therein.

These types of short narrative documents can often be prepared ahead of time, with any updates in tandem with evolution of the clinical program. Perforce, submissions lacking this basic information on the program upfront cannot be scientifically sound.

TABULAR SUMMARIES
THAT COMPILE INFORMATION

Other supportive documents that can often be prepared early—or at least drafted—include tabular summaries. These documents, whose formats are often stipulated by the FDA or other regulatory agencies, provide a concise tabulation for reviewers of the main parameters and results of submitted trials. In essence, tabular summaries serve as a springboard from which reviewers can access specific documents.

Tabular summaries typically partition into groups by category of trial, for example:

- Clinical pharmacology trials (NDA Section 8C)
- Controlled clinical trials (NDA Section 8D)
- Uncontrolled clinical trials (NDA Section 8E)
- Other trials and information (NDA Section 8F)

Other sections besides the clinical section (Item 8) contain tabulated breakdowns by trial category.

The key to efficiently producing these tabulated summaries is twofold: first, agree on the table template, to avoid late-stage debates on format; second, ensure consistency across tabulations to facilitate melding for overview documents, such as the integrated summaries (see Chapter 8, "Overview and Summary Documents").

Early agreement on the format for tabulated summaries cannot be overemphasized. While the advantages of early templating might seem obvious, internal contributors can often lose perspective on the consistency needed across tabulations. Hence, without early agreement, the medical writer often expends considerable energy in defending proposed formats. Furthermore, as shown in Table 9.1, tabulated summaries require decided choices of design, so that required information can be presented to regulatory reviewers in a user-friendly fashion.

Although agency guidelines may differ for stipulated information across categories of trials, the basic information allows a common framework to be constructed. Electronic publishing and other technological systems (see Chapter 5, "Publishing and Information Technology") increasingly support clever table designs. For example, the common table framework could include columnar headings for all trial categories, with individual summaries customized with additional columns by preprogrammed modification. Moreover, similar electronic programs would allow the melding of discrete tabular summaries for overview documents. Such intelligent table construction typifies the underlying strategy (now termed the Emergent Dossier) for regulatory submissions, as discussed in more detail in Chapter 10, "Dossiers for International Projects."

The medical writer for a drug submission thus brings valuable skills to these otherwise mundane tabulations: clever design, electronic tools, and comprehensive perspective all benefit the timely completion of these required sections of a regulatory submission.

INVESTIGATOR'S BROCHURE FOR CLINICAL RESEARCH

Despite this classification as supportive, the Investigator's Brochure (IB) truly defies categorization. According to the ICH (International Conference on Harmonization), the IB represents a compilation of nonclinical and clinical data about the investigational drug. This information allows clinical-trial investigators to enroll subjects in an informed manner, as well as to augment their understanding of the rationale for the protocol and its inherent requirements (U.S. Department of Health and Human Services, 1997).

Thus, the IB initially appears to be a regulatory document; in fact, periodic updates to the drug's IND include any updated IB version (see Chapter 2, "Overview of Drug Development"). However, the IB

TABLE 9.1. Example of a Tabular Summary for Controlled Clinical Trials

Identification: protocol #; investigator(s); publication(s)	Start and complete dates (or status, if ongoing)	Location of full research report and case report forms	Trial design	Duration of trial treatments	Treatment and doses	Formulations of treatments	Subjects per treatment group	Age range (median)	Demographic groups (%); Race (W/B/O); Sex (M/F)
Trial 1: Sanchez P, Jones HL; None	Started 01/01/96; ongoing as of 12/31/96	Report in Volumes 125-129; forms in Volumes 332-335	Double-blind, parallel-group, randomized, placebo-controlled	4 weeks of pretreatment; 40 weeks of active treatment; 4 weeks of follow-up	Drug X: 10 mg 25 mg 50 mg Placebo (twice-daily oral)	Formulations: X-10 X-25 X-50 P-0	25 26 24 25 (100 total)	27-46 (33) 25-52 (36) 22-50 (32) 23-49 (35)	74/11/15; 44/56 68/21/11; 42/58 77/18/05; 51/49 73/17/10; 47/53
Trial 2: Liu HH; *Int Clin J* 1997; 10(2):41-49	Started 04/01/96; completed 08/31/96	Report in Volume 130; forms in Volumes 336-337	Single-blind, randomized, active-controlled	2 weeks of pretreatment; 4 weeks of active treatment; 2 weeks of follow-up	Drug X: 25 mg; Drug Y: 10 mg (twice-daily oral)	Formulations: X-25 Y-10	20 20 (40 total)	21-27 (25) 22-26 (24)	61/29/10; 74/26 65/23/12; 71/29
Trial X (etc.).									

W/B/O = White/black/other
M/F = Male/female

can also be considered a publication document, as it reaches the wider community of investigators, rather than only being submitted to a regulatory agency. And the IB straddles various disciplines of drug development, not unlike an overview document! But, given its relationship to the investigator's ability to conduct a sound clinical trial, the IB more sensibly fits within the category of supportive materials for regulatory submissions.

Information included within an IB grows along with the investigational drug. For the first version of an IB to allow clinical trials in humans, only nonclinical information typically is available. (Unlike the U.S. FDA, some European agencies permit limited clinical trials in human volunteers before an IB would be required more widely.) As nonclinical data grow, and especially as clinical research progresses, considerable new information accumulates that investigators require to conduct trials. Even after marketing, a drug may continue through additional trials within special patient populations or new therapeutic indications. Thus, the drug's sponsor must periodically review an IB to determine if an update of certain sections—or perhaps a fully new edition—is appropriate. Periodic reviews should thus be timed with annual IND filings, as well as with key development milestones, such as completion of Phases I, II, or III.

Table 9.2 delineates sections and information typically included within an IB. Because an IB must be accessible to investigators, the medical writer's skills in organization and clarity contribute to its success. Experts for each section's discipline, however, provide the scientific knowledge key to this dynamic document. The medical writer thus works across research departments to construct a sound IB.

Moreover, within initial construction and subsequent updates of an IB, the writer finds exciting challenges in technologies for document compilation and management. If other documents use standard templates, specific parts can be electronically lifted into appropriate IB sections. For example, the upfront summary of a clinical trial report (see Chapter 7, "Foundation Reports of Research Trials") can be tailored to fulfill the format and information needs of the IB's clinical section. This strategic concept of intelligent development and reuse of documents forms the foundation of Part II's final chapter, "Dossiers for International Projects."

TABLE 9.2. Typical Sections Within an Investigator's Brochure

Section[a]	Contents[b]
Title Page	Identity of drug and sponsor; IB date; confidentiality statement
Table of Contents	Navigational tool for IB user
Summary	Short (2-page) synopsis of highlights across all IB sections
Introduction	Overview of drug, research program, and therapeutic indications
Physical, Chemical, and Pharmaceutical Properties	Description of drug, active components, and relevant properties
Nonclinical Pharmacology	Therapeutic action of drug in animal models
Toxicology	Safety findings identified through stipulated animal studies
Nonclinical Pharmacokinetics and Drug Metabolism	Biotransformation and disposition of drug in animal models
Clinical Pharmacology and Pharmacokinetics	Therapeutic action, biotransformation, and disposition in humans
Clinical Trials	Efficacy, safety, and other findings from available clinical trials
Product Information	Data and findings relevant to current or potential drug labeling
Bibliography	Published literature on the drug, regardless of sponsorship

[a] Adapted from U.S. Department of Health and Human Services, 1997
[b] Refer to current guidelines and company procedures for definitive list of IB sections and subsections
IB = Investigator's Brochure

Chapter 10

Dossiers for International Projects

A stand can be made against invasion by an army;
no stand can be made against invasion by an idea.

—Victor Hugo

As drug research becomes increasingly competitive, international firms must internally collaborate through shared documents. Not only do documents from a single discipline increasingly require input from or review by other departments, but such documents may also be used as source—or even cannibalized—materials. With competitive pressures forcing pharmaceutical companies to produce high-quality submissions in heretofore unprecedented time frames, ongoing initiatives target a dossier approach to expedite regulatory submissions for international drug development.

ACCELERATION OF DRUG DEVELOPMENT

Today's public demands safe and effective drugs to widen the armamentarium of the health practitioner. In fact, modern society often considers access to pharmaceutical products, as part of overall health care, as a basic human right (Bonk, Myers, and McGhan, 1995). Given the often circuitous and commensurately expensive route leading from drug discovery to marketing, opportunities for increased efficiency and international collaboration loom paramount (Blake and Ratcliffe, 1991).

Avenues for increasing efficiency of drug development certainly include expediency in the regulatory submission process. So, as key crafters of the submission package, the medical writer now commands greater prominence, albeit with greater pressure! What can the medical writer do to augment the submission process? In addition to the ways discussed in previous chapters of Part II, the medical writer can also assist, if not lead, initiatives in creating the currently en vogue "Emergent Dossier."

REGULATORY SUBMISSIONS
AS AN EMERGENT DOSSIER

Discrete sections of a drug submission are often referred to as "dossiers", especially among European agencies. Thus, all information filed with the clinical item of an NDA could be termed the "Clinical Dossier"; other items would be similarly named. Hence, the second part of this new term is now defined.

The first part of "emergent," though, does not stem from regulatory jargon. Rather, this term reflects the dynamic development of information contained within a dossier. Data listings, full reports, and other documents start as individual pieces, grow as the clinical program proceeds, and build the pyramidal submission structure (see Chapter 6, "Structure of Regulatory Submissions"). With modern technologies (see Chapter 5, "Publishing and Information Technology"), a regulatory package becomes an "Emergent Dossier" (Figure 10.1).

In fact, the term perhaps first originated with the U.S. FDA's collaborative efforts with the pharmaceutical industry to expedite reviews and approvals for new agents targeting life-threatening diseases, such as AIDS (The Food & Drug Letter, 1994). Modern reliance on international collaboration for research programs and document creation reinforces this now accepted term within the drug and communication industries.

MEDICAL WRITERS AND THE EMERGENT DOSSIER

Where do medical writers fit into the growth of an Emergent Dossier? Actually, the medical writer plays an integral role throughout this full process. Expedited document processes rely on *communication* experts who build submissions with contributions from clinicians, biometricians, and other *technical* experts. As for any technology, the tool is only as helpful as the artisan who uses it; and the craft of medical writing brings the needed artisan to drug development.

FIGURE 10.1. Regulatory Submission as an Emergent Dossier

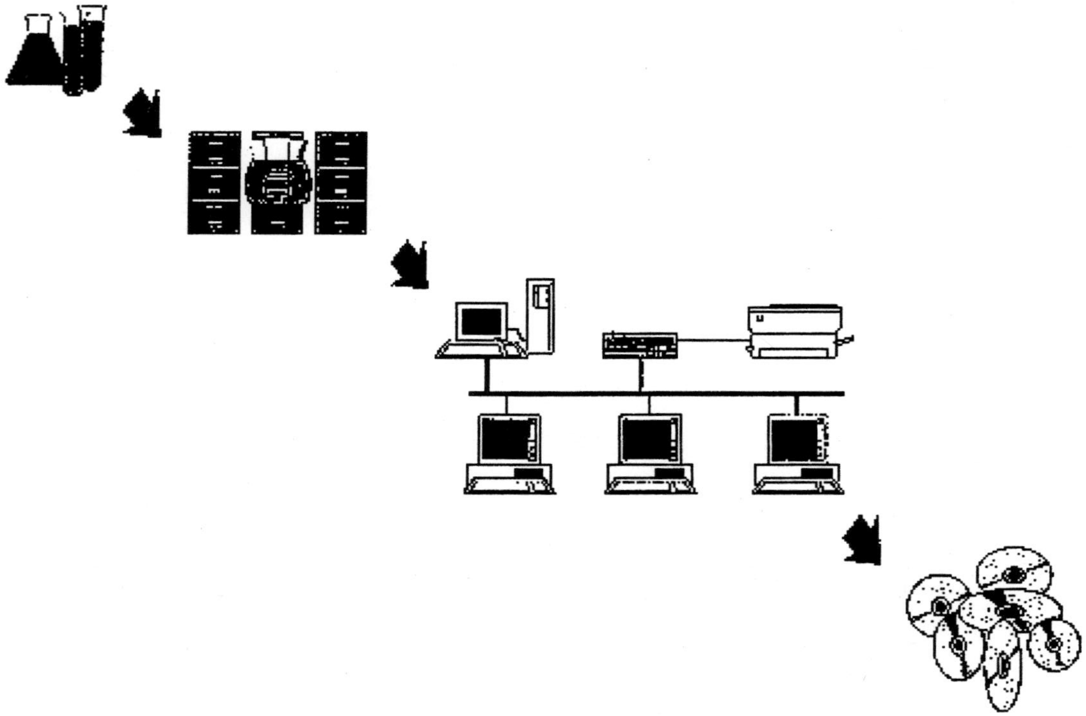

Just as information explodes throughout all of modern society, sophisticated technology to tame this overwhelming outburst leaps from the specialist's drawing board into the portfolio of skills for the medical writer. Electronic publishing, for example, provides a means to integrate and format the reams of text, data, and images comprising a submission (see Chapter 5, "Publishing and Information Technology").

The newer level of tools that underlie concepts like the Emergent Dossier, however, must leap even further forward. Now, mechanisms are needed to facilitate the sharing of information on an international basis, reusing of documents with electronic ties that cross-link sections for automatic updates, and restructuring of component pieces into regulatory submissions tailored to specific agencies.

Furthermore and most critically, document-management systems to ensure version control must enmesh the entire submission web. A daunting task, perhaps, but one crucial for expediting the development of new drugs for better health care.

To be true to our profession, we medical writers must remain at the forefront of modern technologies for information creation, electronic publishing, document management, and other tools only now being realized. Complex, intertwined blueprints for the design and implementation of these document-management systems belie the underlying knowledge of information crucial to the system's success.

The adage that a tool is only as good as the craftsperson is true. Hence, the medical writer must ensure that systems to build an Emergent Dossier will meet the needs of our customers and ourselves. This is our responsibility as writers. And our future.

PART III:
PUBLICATION DOCUMENTS
FOR THE MEDICAL COMMUNITY

Complementing regulatory submissions, publications package research findings into persuasive documents for the external medical community. Part III discusses the vast array of publication documents targeting today's healthcare professionals.

Chapter 11

Rhetorical Strategy for Publications

*In youth men are apt to write more wisely
than they really know or feel.*

—Nathaniel Hawthorne

Throughout Part II, "Regulatory Documents for Drug Submissions," the medical writer's approach emphasizes presenting huge amounts of information from complex research programs to regulatory agencies. In essence, that medical writer plays directly to a captive audience (as in Chapter 6, "Structure of Regulatory Submissions").

Unlike regulatory submissions, however, publication documents do not have a captive audience for bulky dossiers. Instead, publication documents highlight key information in size-constrained formats for the wider medical community of healthcare practitioners, for whose attention many external stimuli compete. Hence, medical writers must hook audiences by deliberately capturing their attention. This chapter introduces rhetorical strategies, along with authorship and ethical issues, in packaging publications for the external medical community.

TYPES OF PUBLICATION DOCUMENTS

The types of publication documents prepared by medical writers vary as much as their potential audiences in the wider medical community. Broadly, three categories emerge:

1. Manuscripts in scientific journals (Chapter 12)
2. Materials for professional meetings (Chapter 13)
3. Promotional pieces and advertising (Chapter 14)

As explored in these topic chapters, each category can include a diversity of specific document types. Materials for professional meetings (Chapter 13), for example, may range from the basic abstract submitted for approval; through posters, slides, or oral presentations at the meeting itself; to compendia of proceedings from the conference. Although related, each subtype relies on deliberate application of effective rhetorical techniques for the document's message to hit its target.

Moreover, the broadening social fabric of modern healthcare weaves new challenges for medical writers, particularly for publication documents. Chapter 15 ("Challenges of Broadening Audiences") identifies some of these new document types. Pharmaceutical economics, for example, now complements traditional research areas of efficacy and safety (Chapter 1, "Basic Introduction to Medical Writing"). Hence, rhetorical strategies must hook the correct audience for each of these broadening document topics.

HOOKING THE EXTERNAL AUDIENCE

The external medical community is a voluntary audience for medical writing. By not being compulsory reading, the successful publication, in fact, must penetrate four rings of audience selectivity to reach its goal (Severin and Tankard, 1988):

1. Selective *perception*—How does each recipient view the message?
2. Selective *exposure*—Will a recipient avoid potential sources of dissonance?
3. Selective *attention*—Do self-fulfilling data capture more notice?
4. Selective *retention*—Will attitudes and beliefs influence later recall?

For illustration, consider a journal manuscript of a clinical trial for hypertension therapy. A family practitioner may *perceive* this information as a way to tailor drug or nondrug therapies to recalcitrant patients, whereas an insurance administrator may worry that externally funded research might be unintentionally biased. A gerontologist satisfied with safety profiles of current therapies might limit *exposure* to possible contradictions by new findings, with the converse true for a researcher. This manuscript, along with others on different topics in a medical journal, would most likely capture *attention* of a cardiologist dealing with hypertension, although an oncologist might skip to articles on cancer treatment. Finally, the nurse interested in nondrug treatments would most likely *recall* statistics on the benefits of diet and exercise, which might be less memorable to the pharmacist firmly believing in drug intervention.

The medical writer, therefore, must consider all four rings of selectivity in packaging these research findings for an external audience (Figure 11.1). The first step, of course, is audience analysis. Once armed with this fundamental information, choices for style, lead-in titles and sentences, level of complexity, visual cues, and other rhetorical techniques logically follow. Deliberate selection of techniques within an overall rhetorical strategy for the document brings to fruition those benefits to be contributed by the medical writer.

AUTHORSHIP AND ETHICAL ISSUES

Benefits that the medical writer contributes to the publication document surpass those directly linked to rhetorical prowess. Through astute cognizance with authorship and other ethical issues, the medical writer safeguards the integrity of the document, not to mention the health of a patient whose treatment decisions might be influenced by the published material. And although not responsible for the conduct of the research, the medical writer *is* responsible for ensuring that the quality of the final document merits publication (Pakes, 1993).

But perhaps the most contentious issue in the "publish or perish" world of professional research is authorship. Standing for far more than peripheral support, true authorship signifies involvement with the research findings commensurate with responsibility for dissemination (McLellan, 1995). As an ethical communicator, the medical writer must be fully aware of authorship conventions, such as promulgations by the International Committee of Medical Journal Editors (1993). The writer must also be prepared to query and even challenge inappropriate authorship attributions. And medical writ-

FIGURE 11.1. Audience Selectivity for Publications

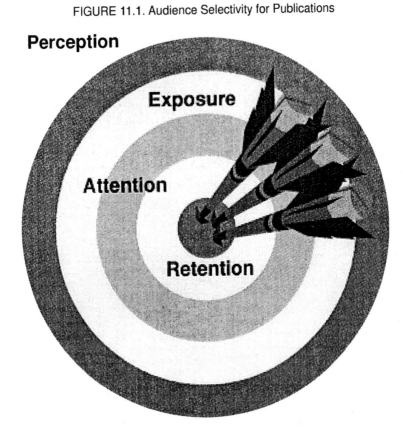

ers must recall that their typical contributions to the final document, albeit hefty, do not constitute full authorship, but rather a well-deserved acknowledgment. (That is, unless the medical writer also significantly contributed to the research itself.)

Other ethical issues similarly can arise during preparation of any publication document. The layout of a poster, for example, could minimize attention to findings contradictory to the original hypothesis; or a three-dimensional graph might accentuate an otherwise inconsequential difference in efficacy outcome between placebo and active treatments. The following chapters raise such ethical issues pertinent to the various categories of publication documents.

Chapter 12

Manuscripts in Scientific Journals

Blessed is the man who, having nothing to say,
abstains from giving wordy evidence of the fact.

—George Eliot

Among broad categorizations of publication documents targeting the external medical community, manuscripts for scientific journals clearly dominate the typical workload for the medical writer. Publication of research findings as a full article within a reputable journal represents a key recognition of the researcher's efforts. Moreover, journals are the mainstay medium for public dissemination of research findings.

Though constraining for specified formats and editorial styles, journals challenge the medical writer to tailor persuasive manuscripts to specific audiences. This chapter explores key aspects of manuscript preparation, identifies alternative formats for journal submissions, and discusses ethical issues for journal manuscripts. Supplementing this information, an appended template provides a working model for preparing a typical journal manuscript from research findings.

KEY ASPECTS OF MANUSCRIPT PREPARATION

All researchers value journal manuscripts. Researchers publish findings to engender professional recognition and to propagate scientific knowledge. In striving for faster development of new drugs, pharmaceutical researchers have come to rely increasingly on medical writers to support this key activity. Hence, medical writers themselves must become the experts regarding manuscript preparation.

The journal manuscript represents the primary publication of findings from a research study, such as a clinical trial. Its status as primary carries weight: it must be the first public dissemination providing peers with enough information to assess the results, repeat the experiments, and evaluate the interpretation (Day, 1994).

Professionals conversant with scientific research recognize the abbreviation "IMRAD" as a mnemonic device for the major sections of a journal manuscript (Iles, 1994):

> I = Introduction (Why was this research undertaken?)
> M = Methods (How was it conducted?)
> R = Results (What was found?)
> A = And (Obviously not a section, but a mnemonic connector!)
> D = Discussion (What do the findings mean? Why are they important?)

The IMRAD format provides a common trellis, established through the past centuries of scientific research, on which to cultivate the manuscript. Audiences of journal readers expect this format; indeed, with few exceptions, journal editors and publishers demand it. Other constraints of the publishing world also affect manuscript preparation: overall length should not exceed a certain level (e.g., five to ten printed pages); conventions for text, tables, figures, and references must be strictly followed; and level of detail must match the intent of each major section (Figure 12.1).

Consider, for example, a manuscript of a clinical trial. The Introduction must place the research hypotheses in proper perspective, but not rehash all details since the advent of penicillin. The Methods, however, must provide sufficient details about trial design, patient groups, compared treatments, and statistical tests so that the research can be scrutinized and potentially replicated. Contrary to common belief, the Results should be relatively succinct in stating the findings; use of tables and graphs, while occupying volume, add great depth. Save interpretation of the findings to the Discussion, in which the findings can be juxtaposed against the original hypotheses—with conclusions.

Furthermore, other sections not identified by this IMRAD convention include the title, abstract, acknowledgment, references, and perhaps others, depending on the journal. Appendix C provides a

FIGURE 12.1. Matching the Level of Detail to the Manuscript Sections

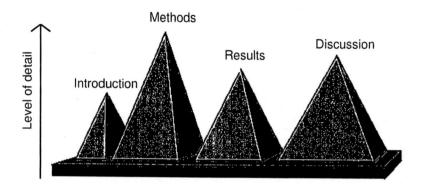

manuscript template, based on standards of the International Committee of Medical Journal Editors (1993). Other texts (e.g., Day, 1994; Spilker, 1991) further delineate preparation of journal manuscripts.

ALTERNATIVE FORMATS FOR JOURNAL SUBMISSIONS

In addition to the standard IMRAD format, publication manuscripts can be constructed in alternative formats, depending on the underlying purpose (Gastel, 1994). Typical categories for involvement of medical writers include review articles, case reports, and letters to the editor. Familiarization with the differences of these alternative formats, relative to the full manuscript, allows the medical writer to advise authors about optimal formats for the intended publication (Table 12.1).

If the manuscript equates to findings of one research trial, then the review article and case report can be considered extreme forms along a continuum. The review article synthesizes findings from other established publications into a comprehensive view of a particular drug treatment, disease area, or other medical issue. In contrast, the case report provides a mechanism to communicate topical findings from one subject in a trial or from one patient under treatment. Formats for a review article depend on its focus: a modifica-

TABLE 12.1. Comparison of Alternative Publication Formats

Alternative format	Comparison with primary journal manuscript	
	Similarities	Differences
Review article	Focus on scientific findings, with their interpretation and importance	Comprehensive view of a particular research area, rather than of one research trial
Case report	Contribution to medical information, with similar format sections	Highlighted findings for one clinical case, rather than for all subjects in a trial
Letter to the editor	Although varied, topic can be the findings from a research trial	Scope much smaller (e.g., specific finding), and topic may be other than a trial per se

tion of IMRAD format may be suitable in some cases, but a series of chapters may better serve at times. The case report can use an abbreviated IMRAD format, but substituting a "Case Description" for both Methods and Results.

The letter to the editor is the wild card, though. Its topics can vary from brief findings from a research trial (not unlike a journal manuscript), to comments on the findings of another researcher's publication, and sometimes to a short essay or commentary piece.

Choosing the most suitable format for a publication document, in addition to the most appropriate journal, increases chances that the submitted document will be accepted for publication (McCann, 1990). Given that publication commands prime importance in the research profession, including the drug industry, the astute medical writer can be a valuable consultant on the appropriate format for a journal submission.

ETHICAL ISSUES FOR JOURNAL MANUSCRIPTS

In addition to general issues of publication ethics (see Chapter 11, "Rhetorical Strategy for Publications"), particular ethical issues relate specifically to authors (and therefore medical writers) of journal manuscripts. By targeting the external medical community, publications must be subject to strict ethical criteria. The complexity of such issues precludes full discussion herein; detailed information can be easily found in separate books, such as recent conference proceedings of the Council of Biology Editors (Bailar, 1990). Instead, a noninclusive list of notable ethical issues follows:

1. *Ownership of data*—Are data the legal property of the author for a funded trial? What if the author and sponsor differ in interpretation?
2. *Redundant publication*—What effects do the hidden repetition of findings in supposedly distinct research trials have on biased propagation of knowledge?
3. *Negative findings*—Do less-glamorous results of "no effect" hinder publication, even though such findings can greatly contribute to scientific research?
4. *Fraud and misconduct*—What are the safeguards to obviate, and the measures to rectify, any publications of untrue findings?
5. *Informed consent*—How were potential risks disclosed to subjects before their agreement to participate in the research?

Many of these ethical issues, along with others not listed above, receive a good dose of preventive medicine through a publication mainstay known as "peer review" (Rennie, 1991). In this key process, primary journal manuscripts must be reviewed, not only by the journal editor, but also by a select group of peers from the scientific community. For example, a manuscript describing the efficacy and safety of a new drug for asthma might be separately reviewed by three to five pulmonologists or related experts, as adjuncts to the internal review by the publishing house. Input from these peers would be considered in judgments of overall quality, scientific integrity, and publication merit of the manuscript.

Of course, the peer-review process itself is not always popular: This external review can increase the time and cost of each publication. But as a safeguard for the ethics and quality of scientific knowledge, peer review's benefits exceed these costs. To augment peer review, however, writers must remain aware of these ethical issues for journal manuscripts. In this way, the writer not only supports authors of manuscripts, but also publishers and readers alike.

Chapter 13

Materials for Professional Meetings

Talking is like a hydrant in the yard
and writing is a faucet upstairs in the house.
Opening the first takes all the pressure off the second.

—Robert Frost

In the fast-paced world of drug research, scientists cannot always wait for journals to publish the latest findings. Journals may represent the greatest volume and highest prestige for external publications, but meetings sponsored by professional societies provide quicker access to external audiences.

Without the lagtimes necessary with peer-reviewed journals, research findings can be brought to the medical community at the numerous conferences held on general and speciality topics. Such professional meetings involve an array of document types: from abstracts submitted for acceptance, through slides and posters at the meeting, ending with proceedings of the overall conference. By deftly using materials for professional meetings, medical writers can present up-to-the-minute research against otherwise daunting deadlines.

ABSTRACTS SUBMITTED FOR ACCEPTANCE

Opportunities abound for all researchers to pursue presentation of their findings at conferences or meetings of professional or technical societies. Some conferences reflect a more catholic approach. For example, the American Medical Association and the American Academy for the Advancement of Science encompass wide scopes of medical or scientific topics, respectively. This latitude, though, incurs more competition among potential presenters. In contrast, specialist societies for compartmentalized disciplines, such as the American Society of Clinical Oncologists, give better odds of acceptance within one's discipline—although subject to the group's own standards.

Unless individually invited to make a presentation, most researchers submit abstracts from which the professional society selects presenters (Eastman and Klein, 1994). In general, the abstract for a professional meeting retains great similarity in content and format to that of a journal article (see Appendix C to Chapter 12, "Manuscripts in Scientific Journals"). Rather than intending to hook a reader of the journal, the meeting abstract serves three primary functions:

1. Acceptance of the research for formal presentation at the conference
2. Enticement of conference participants to attend the poster or slide session
3. Documentation of the research for subsequent conference proceedings

The content of the meeting abstract matches that of the journal manuscript, including the typical IMRAD sections of Introduction, Methods, Results, and Discussion. Given its greater isolation from any appended journal manuscript, the meeting abstract must supply sufficient quantitative results to substantiate the findings. Some societies allow brief tabulations of results within the abstract, although this crutch should be avoided whenever possible.

The remaining challenges in preparing the meeting abstract stem from firm constraints on format; in fact, most societies issue mandatory submission forms (Figure 13.1). And violation of any format requirements (even those seemingly trivial to the nonwriter!) can cause outright rejection of an otherwise solid abstract. The format constraints, though, allow compilation of abstracts into meeting compendia without typesetting. Hence, the medical writer of a meeting abstract has only one chance to get it right; any errors will cause either rejection upfront or embarrassment thereafter.

SLIDES AND POSTERS FOR PRESENTATION

Assuming acceptance of the submitted abstract, the medical writer's next assignment would be preparation of the research findings

FIGURE 13.1. Submission Form for an Abstract

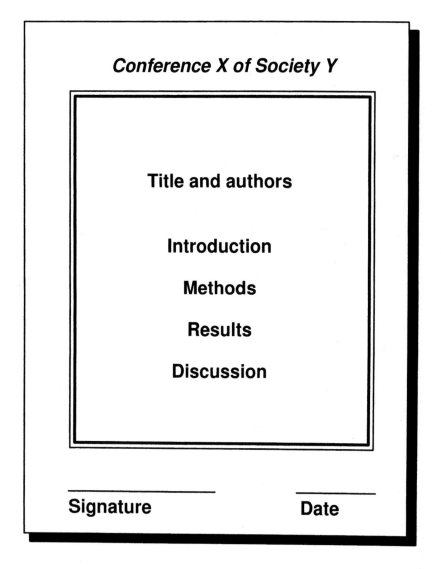

in the format designated by the society. Typically, these formats are either slides that complement a verbal presentation, or a poster displayed within an allotted time and space at the conference. While slides play to a larger one-time audience, posters allow direct interactions with attendees.

Both slides and posters can be viewed as variations of the journal manuscript. In all three cases, the research must cover the IMRAD sections. However, the level of detail and the mechanics of presentation differ greatly among these three formats. Most key is that the journal manuscript can document in considerable detail all major aspects of the research. Moreover, the journal author can explore additional aspects of interest from the research, particularly within the Discussion section.

For both slides and posters, constraints of presentational format limit the level of detail. An oral presentation typically lasts from ten to twenty minutes (Day, 1994a). The presenter therefore must focus the presentation on the main information, saving detailed methods and peripheral findings for another medium (e.g., journal manuscript). Slides visually complement the oral presentation (Figure 13.2), rather than just serving as cue cards. Each slide should emphasize one key message, thereby enhancing comprehension in a few seconds—and avoiding a dozing audience! Given the permanent impression of good slides, and especially poor ones, always use professional services, such as those of a graphics specialist, to prepare the final set of slides.

In contrast to slides, posters do not accompany a scripted presentation (Day, 1994b). Rather, this format presents the research findings as a large freestanding display with dimensions of approximately four feet high by six or eight feet long, albeit at a similar level of detail as for slides. Aesthetic design commands a greater role, however, since the audience will see the full poster at once. An effective poster (Figure 13.3) minimizes text, maximizes graphics, retains white space, and navigates visually. The reader is attracted by the presentation and able to follow the intended thread without distraction. Never risk visibility to cram data: a poster must be readable from about three feet so that a milling crowd does not impede a reader. Once the poster attracts the reader's eye, the presenter can then give additional details, whether verbally or as a

FIGURE 13.2. Construction of a Good Slide

- Use bullets to highlight one key message.
- Complement, don't repeat, the oral presentation.
- Supplement text with tables or graphs.

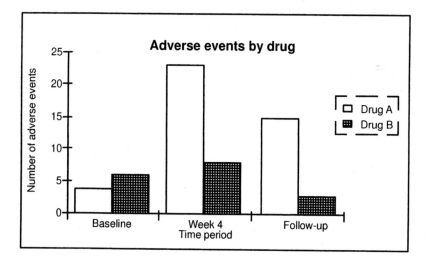

handout. Such individual attention at a more detailed level supplements the formal proceedings that may also be published for the full conference.

PROCEEDINGS OF THE OVERALL CONFERENCE

Many professional societies complete the conference by publishing formal proceedings. These compendia can include detailed agenda of the conference, abstracts submitted for all accepted presentations, transcripts of oral presentations, and, in some cases, abbreviated reports on the research topics. For example, on acceptance, a selected presenter may be invited to submit a report to supplement the slide or poster session. Because conferences facilitate the swiftest dissemination of the latest research, formal pro-

FIGURE 13.3. Design Layout for a Poster

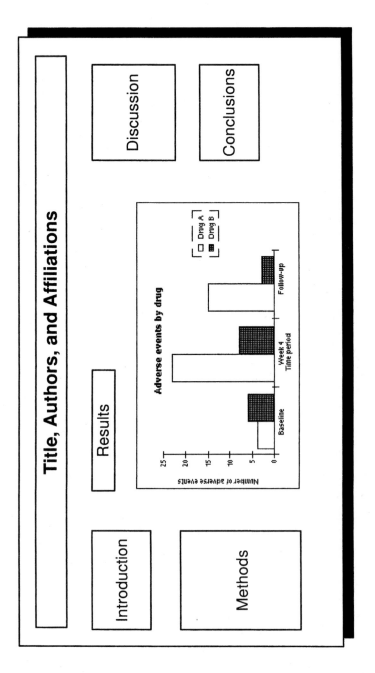

ceedings provide a valuable tool for documenting information at a level beyond that feasible during the meeting.

Medical writers have important roles at both ends of the production of the proceedings. First, professional writers can assist the researcher by developing the initial abstract and presentation into a report according to the conference guidelines. Second, the medical writer or editor may instead be part of the publishing house; in this case, this professional can orchestrate the planning and publishing of proceedings for the overall conference (Smith, 1996). Indeed, report checklists prepared by conference editors can expedite publication (Eastman and Klein, 1991). Integral involvement of medical writers and editors thus ensures proceedings of a professional caliber commensurate with the conference's scientific rigor.

Although formats for conference proceedings can vary by society or publishing house, an abbreviation of the standard IMRAD structure serves as a good basis (Day, 1994c). The conference report thus comprises a brief statement of the research topic, highlights of the methods used, and key results of the research. With fewer constraints than the peer-reviewed journal, proceedings also allow more speculation on full interpretation and wider implications of the findings.

ETHICAL CONCERNS OF REDUNDANT PUBLICATION

Materials for professional meetings are at greater risk for redundant publication than are manuscripts for peer-reviewed journals (Chapter 12, "Manuscripts in Scientific Journals"). The swift publication at conferences invites redundancy. Although not as critical for the submitted abstract versus a proceedings report, redundancy more often occurs as multiple abstracts that are nearly identical in content but submitted to several different conferences.

As professional conferences steadily grow as respected sources for quick publication, greater safeguards against redundancy must be enforced. Abstract forms, for example, almost invariably require formal designation that this information has not and will not be submitted for duplicate publication at another conference. Subsequent development of a journal manuscript, of course, does not constitute redundancy with an initial abstract, although this original source of external publication must be cited. Further clouding the issue of redundancy is the categorization of some conference proceedings as primary publications, which would preclude later submission to a scientific journal (Day, 1994c).

Despite pressures on researchers to "publish or perish", the medical writer must strive to maintain high ethical standards for publications. Too often, researchers keen on ensuring that their findings reach colleagues quickly may simply fail to recognize the critical issues of publication ethics. By fostering better understanding of redundancy for conference materials, the medical writer stands as a bulwark protecting the integrity of scientific knowledge.

Chapter 14

Promotional Pieces for Marketing

In a deep sense, as well as a shallow one,
writing is self-revelatory.

—Robert Penn Warren

Like all healthcare products, drugs occupy their own societal niche. As therapies to foster health and to alleviate illness, drugs are bound by strict government control of their marketing (as discussed in Chapter 2, "Overview of Drug Development"). Yet, drugs are also economic commodities. Besides developing drugs, pharmaceutical companies must manufacture and sell them at a reasonable profit to ensure corporate survival, which includes the potential to develop tomorrow's therapies today.

Within the intersection of societal right and economic good, pharmaceutical products must be marketed to healthcare providers and sold to patients as ultimate consumers. Medical writers contribute to the successful sales and effective marketing of new drugs through preparing promotional pieces for marketing, albeit within the strictest legal and ethical bounds, as explored within this chapter.

PROMOTION WITHIN THE MARKETING MIX

With this century's assimilation of pharmaceutical production into the corporate milieu, the traditional marketing approach has been applied to engender healthy sales, as well as healthy patients (Smith, 1991). This marketing mix, taken from the point of view of the pharmaceutical manufacturer, focuses on the four *P*'s:

1. *Product*—the drug, as well as benefits to the patient using it
2. *Place*—distribution channels, from company to pharmacy to patient

3. *Price*—total cost, not just to the patient, but to the full marketplace
4. *Promotion*—communication of product, place, and price to the patient

A fifth *P* also contributes to the marketing mix in the specific case of a drug:

5. *Position*—differentiation of this product from potential competitors

Position becomes increasingly important with the proliferation of drugs targeting the same therapeutic condition. How does Drug F for hypertension differ from Drugs A to E already on the market? Is its mechanism of action sufficiently different to constitute a new class, such as an angiotensin-converting enzyme inhibitor, rather than a diuretic or a ß-adrenergic blocker? Regardless of class, is a drug's profile of risks versus benefits better for the patient? Or for a specific demographic group, such as the elderly?

Consideration of such questions of position—along with product, place, and price—allows the company to develop a promotion strategy. Indeed, promotion coalesces the other aspects of the marketing mix into communication pieces to inform and persuade the health-care provider as its audience (Figure 14.1). Because promotion focuses on communication through supportive documents, medical writers can be valued members of the marketing team.

SUPPORTIVE DOCUMENTS FOR DRUG PROMOTION

Similar to the marketing mix comprising the five *P*'s, the category of promotion itself can refer to a mix of several types of supportive documents (Smith, 1991). This promotion mix includes several distinct but complementary categories, each with document types of relevance to the writer (Table 14.1). Full examination of these promotion categories remains beyond the scope of this chapter; other references (e.g., Smith, 1991) provide additional information on both marketing overall and promotion specifically. However, a brief overview of those benefits derived from the medical writer gives perspective.

FIGURE 14.1. Drug Promotion Within the Marketing Mix

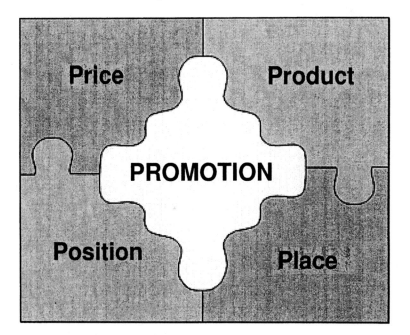

TABLE 14.1. Supportive Documents Within the Promotion Mix

Promotion-mix category	Document type	Typical example
Advertising	Advertisement copy (text); advertisement graphics	Full-page advertisement in a peer-reviewed journal
Personal selling	Journal manuscripts; reference texts	Reprint of a manuscript provided in a sales call
Sales promotion	Training materials; handout materials	Guide on a new drug, to train the sales force
Publicity	Conference materials; lay-press advertising	Published compendium of a sponsored conference

Perhaps the most crucial benefit that the medical writer brings to the promotion mix is a comprehensive view of supportive documents across drug development (Chapter 3, "Types of Pharmaceutical Documents"). Drugs can be promoted only for indications that are approved by regulatory agencies; hence, promotional pieces must be supported by the drug label and its underlying regulatory documents. Manuscripts derived from the research reports can also be used to support promotional statements. Furthermore, each statement within a promotional piece must be technically defensible, especially those involving competitors' products. Understanding the full scope of documents for a drug program therefore remains paramount to an effective promotion mix.

Who better than the medical writer to provide a comprehensive view of this vast arena of supportive documentation? And to prepare the individual documents?

ETHICAL AND LEGAL CONSTRAINTS ON PROMOTION

Because every drug has a balance of benefits and risks for the individual patient, the promotion of pharmaceutical products is strictly regulated. Journal advertisements, for example, must also include key information from the approved labeling to obviate any untoward semblance of promoting unapproved indications (Spilker and Cuatrecasas, 1990). Guidance on promotional restrictions exist for the United States (Pines, 1993), as well as for the European Community and other international territories (Krause and Eldin, 1993). Restrictions also apply to the company's involvement with disseminating reprints of efficacy trials and reference texts.

Even with these regulatory constraints, the medical writer must be vigilant in ensuring that promotional pieces represent fair and unbiased—albeit persuasive—messages. Not only is this an ethical consideration, but a practical one: the avoidance of litigation. As the healthcare industry evolves, the medical writer undoubtedly will slant documents to target the patient directly, rather than indirectly through the provider. The next and final chapter reviews this issue and other challenges to the medical writer within today's malleable healthcare environment.

Chapter 15

Challenges of Broadening Audiences

If there is no struggle, there is no progress.

—Frederick Douglass

Health care remains a basic tenet of our society, whether in the worlds of yesterday, today, or tomorrow; or whether on local, national, or international bases for provision. Throughout the international healthcare milieu, public attention broadens audiences for documents crafted by medical writers. Patient-education materials, health-economic assessments, and electronic journals provide ongoing challenges in medical writing. Such opportunities for the medical writer of tomorrow bring this book to its close.

NEW TOPICS AND NEW MEDIA FOR NEW AUDIENCES

Medical writers must broaden along with health care. New areas of research engender new topics for documents, and sometimes new media for new audiences. Just as medical writing ignited from the spark of medical breakthroughs (see Chapter 1, "Basic Introduction to Medical Writing"), new flames burn as our technological society fans this current fire. And so it should be.

Once, it was enough for the medical writer to know biology, chemistry, pharmacology, and other life sciences. Soon, writing, rhetoric, and language fortified this foundation. Now, previously undreamed disciplines provide niches for specialist writers, although even the generalist must maintain conversance with these and other topics:

- *Biotechnology*—the marriage of body and machine (Foote and Flynn, 1993)
- *Cost-effectiveness*—a tool to value these costly advances (Siegel et al., 1996)

Furthermore, audiences extend from regulatory agencies to the medical community, and finally to patients themselves. Education of the patient, for example, requires specific materials sculpted to reach this diverse audience:

- *Patient-education materials*—translations for the lay public (Cox, 1989)
- *Computer-oriented media*—conduits that reach the target (Angel, 1988)

Consider, for example, the medical writer's role for a new test kit that detects a marker for a genetic disease. First, the test kit depends on biotechnological applications of molecular biology. Second, economists must assess potential benefits of detecting this marker against the cost to develop and use the kit. Third, instructional materials that educate the patient at risk for the disease must be factually honest, yet understandable and unalarming. Fourth, explanation of the underlying biotechnological basis may best be presented through interactive graphics or videos.

Who would have foreseen such advances in techniques and technologies for health care and in communication? Moreover, who can afford not to see them now?

ETHICAL RESPONSIBILITY FOR THE PROFESSION

With this sight comes ethical responsibility. Expanding topics, widening media, and broadening audiences position the medical writer as more than a communicator. Indeed, by influencing behaviors toward healthcare practice and policy, the medical writer now becomes an agent of social change (Gray, 1994). The medical writer no longer just reports facts for a target audience. Through creative documents using modern media, the medical writer can also persuade that audience toward a given action: better diet, routine exercise, prenatal care, therapeutic compliance, and so on.

Moreover, the medical writer can influence societal decisions: insurance coverage of new therapies, subsidization levels for the indigent or elderly, funding for new research, allocation of limited resources, and other issues of political fire. Today's age is one of technology—both healthcare and communication. So who better than the medical writer to accept this torch of responsibility for healthcare communication?

APPENDIXES:
TEMPLATES FOR MEDICAL-WRITING DOCUMENTS

Document templates provide the medical writer with standard formats from which to prepare specific pieces, whether for regulatory submissions or external publications. Although templates represent a starting point, the medical writer should always check for specific requirements for content or format that may be mandated by the company sponsor or external agencies. The following three appendixes offer templates that exemplify three of the major document types covered within this book:

1. Foundation report for a clinical research trial (Appendix A)
2. Overview document for a regulatory submission (Appendix B)
3. Publication manuscript for an external journal (Appendix C)

These templates should give both novice and experienced medical writers a level of support along their professional journeys into tomorrow's world of health care.

Appendix A

Template for a Clinical Trial Report

GENERAL GUIDELINES FOR THE REPORT TEMPLATE

This report template details a generic document that could subsequently be modified, as appropriate, for specific issues of regulatory agencies or the sponsoring company, or for the nature of the drug or therapeutic area.

In using this template to prepare a clinical trial report, consider the following points:

1. Provide structure to guide the reader through the report's huge amount of detailed information. This structure takes the form of visible headers, offset from normal text, and following a logical numbering sequence.
2. Double-space the entire document, especially for review drafts. Use bulleted lists and white space to facilitate the reader's comprehension.
3. For lengthy documents, begin each new major section (e.g., Section 1, but not 1.1) on a new page. Short documents may not require such separation of text.
4. Insert tables and figures as close as possible to the text references. Refer to each table and figure included in the report. Support statements with tables or figures that provide quantitative details. Relegate lengthy collections of supportive material to end sections or appendixes.

TRIAL NUMBER AND TITLE

Note that the trial number is determined by an internal algorithm of the sponsor. Use no more than two or three lines of text for a concise title. Reflect key aspects of the trial, including features such as the following:

1. Design (e.g., randomized, blinded, controlled)
2. Therapeutic condition (e.g., hypertension, diabetes, asthma)
3. Patient population (e.g., children versus elderly, women or men, healthy or not)
4. Treatment (e.g., drugs, placebo, or other comparison agents)
5. Length of treatment (e.g., two weeks versus two years)

PAGINATION

Order the material in the report according to the pagination scheme suggested in the following table:

Section	Numbering format	Number on page?
Title Page	Lower-case Roman (i)	No
Summary	Lower-case Roman (ii–?)	Yes
Table of Contents	Lower-case Roman	Yes
List of Tables	Lower-case Roman	Yes
List of Figures	Lower-case Roman	Yes
List of Appendixes	Lower-case Roman	Yes
Text	Arabic (1–?)	Yes
Appendixes	Letter/Arabic (e.g., A1)	Yes

COVER PAGE

TRIAL NUMBER: TRIAL TITLE

Key Dates:

    Trial initiated   ⸻

    Trial completed   ⸻

    Trial terminated   ⸻   *(if appropriate)*

    Report issued   ⸻

Principal Investigator:

    Name: ⸻

    Affiliation (e.g., institution and address): ⸻

⸻

Sponsor Contact(s):

    Name: ⸻

    Telephone number: ⸻

⸻

TABLE OF CONTENTS

Provide a full table of contents for the entire report. List all sections, tables, figures, and appendixes. This format provides a typical example. To facilitate preparation, use a separate scheme (e.g., lower-case Roman numerals) for pages preceding the main body of text for the report.

SUMMARY

TRIAL NUMBER: TRIAL TITLE

OBJECTIVES

METHODS

Trial design

Target population

Treatment dosage

Main assessments

Statistical considerations

RESULTS

Demography

Efficacy

Pharmacokinetics *(or other assessments)*

Safety

CONCLUSIONS

Summarize the report, preferably within two pages. Focus on key aspects of the trial, including primary objectives, main design, principal results, and overall conclusions. Rely on text descriptions; substitute succinct tables when more concise, particularly for presentation of results. The summary should stand alone from the main report.

TRIAL NUMBER: TRIAL TITLE

1   INTRODUCTION

1.1   Background

Highlight key information about the drug, its intended therapeutic use, and the purpose and design of the trial, thereby placing the drug's clinical development in perspective. Do not exceed one paragraph, unless the situation is exceptional.

1.2   Objectives

State the objectives of the trial as specifically as possible; broad objectives, such as overall efficacy and safety, do not provide sufficient definition for the trial's conduct. If appropriate, distinguish primary objectives that drive the trial's design, from secondary objectives that collect supportive data. Note planned versus exploratory subgroup analyses or any supplemental objectives determined after the protocol was designed.

2   METHODS

2.1   Trial Design

2.1.1   Overview of Trial Structure

Clearly describe the structure of the trial, including the following key characteristics: experimental treatments (e.g., trial drug, comparison agent, placebo); target population; level and method of blinding (e.g., open, single-blind, double-blind); assignment of subjects to groups (e.g., randomized, stratified); and the overall configuration of the trial (e.g., parallel, crossover, sequential). Append the trial protocol and all amendments.

2.1.2   Description of Treatment Periods

Delineate the sequence and duration of specific trial periods, such as baseline, active treatment, crossover washouts, treatment withdrawal, and post-treatment follow-up. Graphically portray the trial structure.

2.1.3 Timing of Assessments

Summarize the timing of efficacy, safety, or other assessments, in relation to the specific structure of the trial. Use a tabular or graphical display.

2.2 Trial Population

2.2.1 Target Population

Define the population of subjects (i.e., healthy individuals) or patients (i.e., subjects with the medical condition), and the number (i.e., size) intended for the trial. (Refer to the section on power calculations [Section 2.6.2], as appropriate.)

2.2.2 Inclusion Criteria

Delineate the characteristics of subjects qualifying them for entry into the trial.

2.2.3 Exclusion Criteria

Delineate the characteristics of subjects *dis*qualifying them from entry into the trial.

2.2.4 Withdrawal Criteria

Define any predetermined criteria causing elimination of subjects after entry into the trial (e.g., noncompliance with treatment, individual choice, adverse events). Clarify any ramifications regarding evaluability of the data from such subjects. (Additional details may be provided within the sections on statistical analyses.)

2.2.5 Concomitant Therapy

Describe the allowance or disallowance of therapies (i.e., drugs other than the trial treatments, or other medical treatments) received concomitantly during the trial. Discuss any issues pertinent to interactions with trial treatments or confounding of results from trial assessments.

2.3   Trial Treatments

2.3.1   Treatment Groups

Define the specific treatments to which subjects were assigned, including active drug treatments, and placebo or other controls. Address any circumstances pertinent to the trial structure (e.g., crossover design) or selection criteria (e.g., subjects previously responding, or not, to specific treatments).

2.3.2   Dose Selection

Specify the selected regimens of each trial treatment, including the amounts, timing, and route of administration. Explain the rationale for dose and dose-interval selection, as needed, with information about dose-response pattern, pharmacokinetic profile, or blood-level response of the trial treatment.

2.3.3   Treatment Compliance

Describe any specific procedures used to monitor or assess compliance with trial treatments (e.g., pill counts, or drug levels in blood or urine samples).

2.4   Assignment Procedures

2.4.1   Group Assignment

Describe the procedures for assigning subjects to specific treatment groups. Include information on randomization, stratification, blocking, or other relevant techniques. If used, a computer-generated randomization schedule should be described, with the actual schedule appended. For a multicenter trial, tabulate this information by center.

2.4.2 Blinding Techniques

Specify any procedures used to ensure subject blinding to treatment in a single-blind trial, or subject and investigator blinding in a double-blind trial (e.g., matched placebo and control tablets, labeling of drug bottles). Address any specific issues about titration of treatments through dose ranges, or handling of particular structural periods (e.g., placebo baseline or washout periods). Justify the lack of blinding techniques, if not employed in the trial (e.g., open-label structure).

2.4.3 Material Identification

List the sources of treatments used in the trial, and the specific lot or batch numbers of these treatments. Describe any modifications to treatments needed for blinding techniques (e.g., recoating of tablets, or grinding of tablets for capsule enclosure).

2.5 Methods of Assessment

Delineate the methods used to assess the results of the trial, in terms of assessments of efficacy, pharmacokinetic, safety, or other criteria relevant to the trial objectives. As appropriate, refer to tabular or graphical displays of the trial design and assessments.

2.5.1 Efficacy

Clearly specify the efficacy end points, and the methods of assessing these end points. Delineate primary end points that drive the trial structure from any secondary end points that allow collection of supportive information.

2.5.2 Pharmacokinetics (or other assessments)

Specify any pharmacokinetic or other assessments pertinent to the trial.

2.5.3 Safety

Describe all methods employed for assessing the safety of subjects participating in the trial. Specify the means used to capture the types and occurrences of adverse events (e.g., volunteered by subject, or elicited through questioning or checklist). Define rating scales or other methods for categorizing adverse events by level of severity or relation to trial treatment. List specific safety tests to be performed (e.g., electrocardiographic monitoring, physical examinations, clinical laboratory measurements), and the criteria used to assess these results (e.g., comparison with control groups or baseline values).

2.6   Statistical Considerations

2.6.1   Statistical Tests and Analytical Plans

Describe the analyses planned for the trial assessments, and specify the statistical tests used in these analyses. Address any issues about handling data from subjects who violated protocol specifications, withdrew prematurely from the trial, or were otherwise deemed unevaluable. Relegate detailed statistical discussions to an appendix.

2.6.2   Power Calculations and Sample Size

Identify the levels of significance, power of analyses, and predetermined sample size.

2.6.3   Interim and Exploratory Analyses

Describe and justify any interim or exploratory analyses not planned in the protocol.

2.7   Administrative Issues

2.7.1   Informed Consent and External Review Boards

Discuss the procedures used for obtaining informed consent of subjects before their participation in the trial. Describe the role of any ethical review boards who reviewed the trial protocol and approved its use at the investigation sites. Identify any external committees who monitored aspects of trial conduct (e.g., safety or data monitoring).

2.7.2   *Quality Assurance and Good Clinical Practice*

List the steps taken at the investigation sites, and by the trial sponsor, to ensure the accuracy, consistency, completeness, and reliability of collected data. Include relevant information on training and monitoring of investigators, use of instructional manuals, methods for data verification, or periodic audits of record files. For multicenter trials, discuss methods used to ensure sufficient standardization across investigation sites. Specify any guidelines or regulations by which the trial was conducted, such as U.S. FDA standards for good clinical practice.

3   RESULTS

The complexity of the protocol determines the most appropriate format for presentation of results. For example, trials involving many assessments, particularly over several time points, may amass too many data to be presented within one hierarchical section. In these cases, subdivide the single *Results* section (3) into separate stand-alone sections, such as *Demography* (3), *Efficacy* (4) and *Safety* (5). Otherwise, the subordination of subsections may become unwieldy.

3.1   *Demography*

3.1.1   *Disposition of Entered Subjects*

Account for all subjects who entered the trial, clearly identifying the number of subjects who completed any baseline period, were assigned to treatments, received treatments, participated in each successive period of the trial's design, completed active treatment, and continued through any follow-up period. Delineate the numbers of subjects, by treatment group, who withdrew from the trial (and the reason), or who deviated from or violated the protocol. Present this hierarchical disposition of entered subjects with a table, flowchart, or other graphical display. Provide a subject-by-subject listing for all subjects prematurely leaving the trial, with information on their assigned treatment, duration of treatment, reason for leaving, and any other pertinent information.

3.1.2   Demographic and Baseline Details

Analyze the critical demographic and baseline characteristics of subjects, along with any additional factors noted during the trial that could affect its outcome. Compare specific treatment groups for similarity, noting any important differences across groups. Use tables and figures to succinctly present demographic details, especially in group comparisons; append individual subject values.

Demographic details to be considered will have been determined by the protocol, in terms of target population and inclusion and exclusion criteria, as relevant to the trial's objectives. Demographic details, however, typically include descriptive factors, such as age, sex, race, and weight; factors about the disease to be treated, such as duration, severity, and baseline assessments for critical clinical variables; characteristics at trial entry, such as concomitant illnesses and therapies; and comparisons across centers, for multicenter trials.

3.1.3   Data Sets for Analyses (if appropriate)

Depending on the disposition of subjects throughout the trial's treatment periods, it may be necessary to consider subsets of subjects for specific analyses, such as an efficacy subset for those subjects completing the full trial versus all randomized subjects in an intent-to-treat analysis. Clearly identify any data sets so determined.

3.2   Efficacy

Overall grouping of efficacy results derives from those assessments stipulated in the protocol. As such, use discretion in determining the number of text subdivisions needed for efficacy results, as well as those headers actually used. For example, consider substituting "Pulmonary Function" for the general header "Primary Assessments" in an asthma trial. Generally, include tables of group summaries or figures of key trends in the main text, but relegate detailed listings of individual subject data to appendixes.

3.2.1   Primary Assessments

Handle as noted above.

3.2.2   Secondary Assessments

Handle as noted above.

3.2.3   Overall Efficacy Evaluation

Synthesize the results of all efficacy analyses into an evaluation of the overall efficacy determined in the trial. Identify any points that obscure this determination, potentially affect subpopulations of subjects, or require additional trials for clarification.

3.3   Pharmacokinetics (or other assessments)

If appropriate to the trial design, present the results of pharmacokinetics or any other assessments (e.g., microbiology). Follow the same general pattern as for efficacy.

3.4   Safety

Describe safety results in sufficient detail for understanding of the drug profiles shown by the trial. Generally, include tables of group summaries or figures of key trends in the main text, but relegate detailed listings of individual subject data to appendixes. Critical safety information, though, may require listings and narratives for individual subjects within the main text, such as for deaths or potentially serious adverse events.

3.4.1   Extent of Exposure

Delineate the extent of exposure to trial treatment for subject groups, including any placebo or comparison agents. Specify information on number of exposed subjects, duration of exposure, and dose. For groups, list mean or median values, or provide a breakdown of the number of subjects exposed for categories of time or dose level. Cumulative doses may also be relevant. Address the elimination from safety analyses of any subjects who received treatment, since all subjects who received at least one dose of trial treatment would usually be included.

3.4.2   Adverse Events

Describe the patterns and rates of occurrence for adverse events noted for treatment groups during the trial; supplement this narrative description with supportive tables and figures. Group adverse events by body system (e.g., gastrointestinal). Break down the adverse events by predefined levels of severity (e.g., mild, moderate, severe), and by treatment relationship (e.g., not related, possibly related, definitely related). Compare the incidences of adverse events across treatment groups and over time, with special regard for those adverse events that did not occur during any baseline period.

Focus on adverse events with high rates or severe levels, in relationship to treatment, or associated with deaths, withdrawals, or dose adjustments. Specifically, tabulate by group the numbers of subjects who died, withdrew from trial treatment, or had serious adverse events; append descriptive narratives of the circumstances of each case.

3.4.3   Clinical Laboratory Tests

Group results of clinical laboratory tests (e.g., biochemistry, hematology, urinalysis). Present findings according to the methods determined in the protocol; typically, such presentations include mean or median values over time; numbers of subjects with changes of a predefined nature (e.g., from baseline value, or of a certain magnitude); and relationship to normal laboratory ranges.

3.4.4   Other Observations (if appropriate)

If appropriate to the trial design, present the results of any other special assessments of safety, particularly as related to the specific drug or target disease being considered (e.g., electrocardiography for a drug with the potential to affect the heart).

3.4.5   Overall Safety Evaluation

Synthesize the results of all safety analyses into an evaluation of the overall safety determined in the trial. Identify any points that obscure this determination, potentially affect subpopulations of subjects, or require additional trials for clarification.

3.5 Discussion (optional)

Typically, results of a clinical trial do not require extensive discussion or comparisons with scientific literature. But as warranted for unusual issues, include a brief section on unexpected findings or results that conflict with established knowledge. Identify the possible underlying reasons and compare with key literature, as appropriate.

4 CONCLUSIONS

Summarize the key findings for the trial. Specifically, state one conclusion for each objective originally or subsequently identified.

5 REFERENCES

List full bibliographic information for all literature references cited within the report. Consistently follow a given format and style. Copies of the specific references may be appended to the report, particularly those references not commonly available.

APPENDIXES

Provide an index to all appended material. Group appendixes by the nature of the material included therein; one grouping scheme follows:

    A. Literature References
    B. Trial Investigators and Curricula Vitae
    C. Trial Protocol and Revisions
    D. Sample Case Report Forms
    E. Randomization Schedules
    F. Publications of Trial Results
    G. Individual Data Listings
    H. Statistical Documentation

For reports of considerable length, consider using a separate page-numbering scheme for appendixes (e.g., A1 for Appendix A, B1 for Appendix B, etc.). Otherwise, revisions to earlier sections may introduce logistical problems with appendixes that would usually be compiled at an earlier stage in report preparation.

APPENDIX A
Literature References

Item	Page
Reference 1	A1
Reference 2	A5

etc.

Provide an index preceding each appendix, using this format as an example.

Appendix B

Template for an Overview Regulatory Document

GENERAL GUIDELINES FOR THE OVERVIEW TEMPLATE

This template for an overview regulatory document presents, as a model, the elements typically required for NDA Section 2H, Clinical Data Summary and Results of Statistical Analysis. As appropriate, revise this template for updated regulatory guidelines and as needed for the specific drug and therapeutic indication.

Points to consider in constructing the research report (see Appendix A) apply to this overview template. Additionally, construct the document with the reader in mind: use navigational techniques and other format tools that assist the agency or other reviewer in following the evidence for each conclusion. Remember that guidelines often offer an additional challenge of brevity; for example, all information required within this template for Section 2H generally must fit within about 150 pages. Use of summary sections of research reports may therefore facilitate construction.

Moreover, this working model exemplifies templates that could similarly be constructed for other overview and summary documents in a regulatory submission.

SECTION 2H:
CLINICAL DATA SUMMARY
AND RESULTS OF STATISTICAL ANALYSIS

1   INTRODUCTION

Provide sufficient background about the clinical program for the drug being studied. Summarize key features of the program, in relation to the analysis of results; avoid redundancy with earlier sections contained within Item 2. Include a short summary of findings from the clinical program, based on information provided in the document's following sections. Preferably, limit the Introduction to one or two pages.

2   CLINICAL PHARMACOLOGY

Provide a description of the methods and key results for the Phase I (or other phase) trials that investigated the absorption, distribution, metabolism, excretion, tolerance, dose-ranging, drug interaction, dependence, or other pharmacological parameters in humans. Include a comparison of findings in humans with those in animals.

2.1   Tabular Summary

Tabulate all trials categorized as clinical pharmacology. Include the following information: protocol identifier; investigator; trial design; comparison agents (if any); and number of subjects, with their age, sex, dose, and duration of dosing.

2.2   Narrative Descriptions

For each trial, provide a short narrative description of its overall design and results. Emphasize tables and figures to effectively present key findings.

2.3   Conclusions

List conclusions from this group of trials. Summarize the critical findings of clinical pharmacology. Highlight those relevant to clinical use of the drug in humans.

3 OVERVIEW OF CLINICAL TRIALS

Briefly describe the overall plan for the clinical program, with particular reference to specific guidelines used or agency-sponsor discussions of key issues. Explain any critical features of the program; e.g., duration of dosing, choice of trial design or control, targeted efficacy benefits or potential adverse events, and determination of safety. As appropriate, include a brief review of pertinent clinical literature and consider findings for related drugs that might assist assessment of this drug.

4 CONTROLLED CLINICAL TRIALS

Provide a description of the methods and key results for all controlled clinical trials for each proposed therapeutic indication and specific efficacy claim for the drug. Include trials regardless of their outcome (i.e., positive, negative, or neutral).

4.1 Tabular Summary

Tabulate all clinical trials categorized as controlled, whether conducted by the sponsor or made available through published or unpublished sources. Include the following information: protocol identifier; reference to any publications; investigator(s); trial design; specific formulation and dosage; comparison agents; number of subjects, with their age, sex, dose, and duration of dosing; and location of the research report in the clinical section of the submission.

4.2 Narrative Descriptions

For each trial, provide a short narrative description that includes enough detail to allow understanding of the trial's design, conduct, analysis, and results, for both efficacy and safety. Describe statistical techniques, specific methods, and any exclusions for subjects. Include quantitative results (i.e., actual values or calculated changes), not just statistical significance. Emphasize tables and figures to effectively present key findings.

4.3 Conclusions

Analyze results and list conclusions from this group of trials, individually and by each claim of efficacy. Defend the rationale for emphasizing any one trial over others. For any analyses of pooled data, explain the reasoning. Identify any major inconsistencies or areas for further research. Discuss specific findings that clarify dose relationships with pharmacological response or duration of action. Especially consider evidence of any differences (efficacy or safety) across demographic (e.g., age, sex, race) or other subgroups (e.g., those with renal or hepatic impairment) of subjects.

5   UNCONTROLLED CLINICAL TRIALS

Provide a description of the methods and key results for all uncontrolled clinical trials. Aim for a level of detail appropriate to the lower importance of this trial category.

5.1 Tabular Summary

Tabulate all clinical trials categorized as uncontrolled. Include the following information: protocol identifier; indication studied; investigator(s); specific formulation and dosage; number of subjects, with their age, sex, dose, and duration of dosing; and location of the research report in the clinical section of the submission. Do not include other published reports unless of substantial size or with notable findings.

5.2 Narrative Descriptions

For each trial, provide a short narrative description of the design and results, for both efficacy and safety. Emphasize tables and figures to effectively present key findings.

5.3 Conclusions

Analyze results and list conclusions from this group of trials. Focus on safety results, but include any areas suggested for further research.

6   OTHER STUDIES AND INFORMATION

Briefly describe any remaining data available that would not be categorized in the previous sections, but that would appropriately supplement safety information. For example, include summaries of such trials (whether controlled or uncontrolled) and papers (published or unpublished) for claims outside of this particular application, for foreign marketing experience, or for epidemiologic data. Although not required, a format similar to the previous sections, albeit in less detail, should be used.

7   SAFETY SUMMARY

Provide a comprehensive overview of the safety profile of the drug. For consistency, use Section 8H, Integrated Summary of Safety Information, as the prime data source.

7.1   *Extent of Exposure*

Describe the extent of exposure for subjects in the clinical program, and the number of subjects exposed to drugs for various periods of time and at various doses.

7.2   *Adverse Events*

Integrate data from the controlled and uncontrolled trials, as previously categorized. Provide estimated rates of adverse events. Tabulate the more important (serious or frequent) events by logical groupings. Present separate analyses for controlled versus open-label trials, and for short-term versus long-term dosing. Specify any differences in rates attributable to dose, duration of dosing, or demographic characteristics. Also identify any potential interactions of this drug with others likely later to be used.

Separately analyze any subjects who prematurely terminated involvement in the trial because of an adverse event or death. Examine possibilities of unexpected adverse events. Determine adverse events of the greatest clinical significance.

Discuss available data for any potentially serious adverse events (e.g., hepatotoxicity, leukopenia, or agranulocytosis), even if not definitively attributed to the drug. Indicate any planned steps (pre-marketing or postmarketing) to further explain the relationship of these adverse events to wider use of the drug.

7.3   *Clinical Laboratory Data*

Summarize data from clinical laboratory analyses (e.g., biochemistry, hematology, or urinalysis). Note any clinically or statistically significant trends in mean values for groups, and markedly abnormal values for individual subjects. Compare the drug with placebo or active agents, as appropriate to the design of the trials; specify the number of tested subjects per group. Identify subjects prematurely terminating involvement in a trial because of clinical laboratory findings, and evaluate their abnormal results in terms of the drug's overall safety profile.

7.4   *Other Safety Assessments*

Consider results of any special safety assessments in the clinical program, such as audiometric tests, electrocardiograms, or ophthalmologic examinations, particularly as relevant to this drug or class of drugs. Include data comparisons with placebo and active agents, as appropriate. Identify the number of tested subjects per group.

7.5   *Overdosage*

Include any available information on the treatment of overdosage with the drug.

7.6   *Drug Abuse*

State whether the drug has the potential to be abused. For a drug subject to abuse, provide a summary of the trials or other relevant information on this potential. For a drug not considered abusable but a member of a drug class known to have abuse potential, discuss reasons if trials of abuse potential have not been included in the clinical program.

7.7 Safety Summary

Summarize key findings that support the identified safety profile of the drug in clinical use. Do not simply repeat findings; rather, integrate related evidence into a coherent and comprehensive view.

8 OVERALL CONCLUSIONS

Weave together the conclusions from the clinical pharmacology trials, controlled trials, uncontrolled trials, other information, and safety results, so as to present an overall profile of the drug's clinical findings. Recapitulate key conclusions. Identify any key issues for particular demographic groups or areas requiring further research. From this Section 2H, build a bridge into its following NDA Section 2I, Discussion of Benefit/Risk Relationship and Proposed Postmarketing Studies.

Appendix C

Template for a Publication Manuscript

GENERAL GUIDELINES
FOR THE MANUSCRIPT TEMPLATE

This manuscript template comprises instructions for the major sections of a primary publication in a medical journal. As appropriate, this model should be revised for updated publication guidelines, especially considering the target journal, and for tailoring the document to specific research types.

Points to consider in constructing the research report (see Appendix A) apply to this manuscript template. Always construct the document for the intended audience: who will be reading this particular journal, and why? Recall that printed space in key journals is limited, and thus presented information must balance thoroughness with brevity. Templates for alternative publication formats, as discussed in Chapter 12, can be derived from this journal format.

PRIMARY JOURNAL MANUSCRIPT

Title

Label the manuscript with a concise but informative title. Readers typically scan titles in the journal's table of contents; hence, the title must contain the main hook to capture the reader's attention. Avoid unnecessary words (e.g., "research," "findings," or "data"). Include key words that will be the primary source for later electronic literature searches. If requested, provide a shorter "running title" to appear on each printed page.

Author(s)

List all qualifying authors for the manuscript, in order of their contributions. Mention other contributors who do not qualify as authors in the Acknowledgments section. Follow journal requirements for use of initials or inclusion of degrees and affiliations. Limit the number of qualifying authors to three (preferably), although some journals allow up to six or eight as a maximum. For collective research, as by a collaborative group, designate one or more key participants as authors, or use a group designation with an identified Chairperson to indicate full public responsibility. Names of other members may be appended or listed in a footnote.

Abstract

Summarize all key aspects of the research study within 250 words total, depending on the journal. Include relevant information from all sections so that the abstract stands alone as a condensation of the manuscript. Provide quantitative results as text; do not use tables or figures. Avoid any literature references. Focus on capturing the attention of those readers hooked by the title so that they then begin reading the full article.

Introduction

Provide sufficient background on the research to place it into perspective for the reader. Cite key references; do not exhaustively review the literature. Identify the purpose of the research, along with the main hypotheses. Guide the reader through the rest of the manuscript. The lead-in sentence must be strong enough to retain reader interest.

Methods

Describe the design and conduct of the research in sufficient detail to allow readers or reviewers to replicate the findings. Cite key references for methods or analyses used. As appropriate to the trial, include statements about ethical treatment of participants. Provide details about experimental design and statistical analyses to support all results.

Results

Simply present the findings of the research. Supplement text with tables and figures. Do not repeat information; rather, use tables to summarize data, figures to show trends or relationships, and text to highlight these findings. Above all else, be accurate!

Discussion

Interpret the findings of the research. Address each hypothesis. Relate findings to the rationale for the research, as stated in the *Introduction* section. Identify any limitations of the research, with their potential effects on data interpretation, as well as potential areas for further research. Compare findings with the established literature. Justify the importance of this research.

Conclusions

Briefly state the conclusions from this research, as linked to the research hypotheses. Do not repeat information from other sections; instead, pull the main findings together. (*Note:* The *Conclusions* section may not be used in all journal formats; if not, insert the conclusions of the research in the final portion of the *Discussion* section instead.)

Acknowledgments

Provide credit to nonauthors who contributed strongly to the research or manuscript. Examples of such contributions include medical writing or editing, technical assistance in the laboratory, and intellectual input. Do not acknowledge too liberally: simply doing one's job (e.g., word processing) is valuable, but not commensurate with formal credit. Always identify any financial support, as well as other relationships that may potentially involve a conflict of interest. Obtain written approval for any acknowledgment from the person cited; be scrupulous with spellings, degrees, titles, and affiliations!

References

Provide bibliographic information for all references cited in the text. Carefully proofread citations for accuracy and completeness. Always follow the specified journal format.

References

Chapter 1

Bazerman, C. (1991). Communicating within the changing social space of medicine today. *AMWA (American Medical Writers Association) Journal* 6(1):18-20.

Berland, T. (1983). The challenge of medical writing in America. *Perspectives in Biology and Medicine* 26(4):587-594.

Bonk, R. J., M. J. Myers, and W. F. McGhan. (1995). Drug expenditures in a balanced strategy for healthcare policy. *PharmacoEconomics* 7(6):534-542.

Losi, M. J. (1987). Scientific writing: The servile profession? *AMWA (American Medical Writers Association) Journal* 2(5):16-17.

Watts, M. S. M. (1987). Medical writers and power: Impact on medicine, health care and the world. *AMWA (American Medical Writers Association) Journal* 2(1):7-11.

Chapter 2

Friedman, L. M., C. D. Furberg, and D. L. DeMets. (1984). *Fundamentals of clinical trials.* See chapter "Introduction to clinical trials." Littleton, MA: John Wright, PSG Inc.

Nightingale, S. L. (1995). Challenges in international harmonization. *Drug Information Journal* 29:1-9.

Pines, W. L. (1981). A primer on new drug development. *FDA Consumer,* HEW Publication No. (FDA) 81-3021, U.S. Department of Health and Human Services, Public Health Services, Food and Drug Administration (FDA).

Smith, C. G. (1992). *The process of new drug discovery and development.* See chapter "Overview of drug discovery and development." Boca Raton, FL: CRC Press, Inc.

Spilker, B., and P. Cuatrecasas. (1990). *Inside the drug industry.* See chapter "Clinical drug development." Barcelona: JR Prous, SA.

U.S. Department of Health and Human Services, Public Health Services, Food and Drug Administration (FDA). (1981). *Clinical testing for safe and effective drugs,* HHS Publication No. (FDA) 74-3015.

Chapter 3

Lamm, C. M. (1994). Rhetoric in science. *AMWA (American Medical Writers Association) Journal* 9(3):89-91.

Orna, E. (1985). The author: Help or stumbling block on the road to designing usable texts? In: *Designing usable texts*, edited by T. M. Duffy and R. Waller. Orlando, FL: Academic Press, Inc.

Severin, W. J., and J. W. Tankard Jr. (1988). *Communication theories: Origins, methods, uses*, Second Edition. See chapter "Perception and communication." White Plains, NY: Longman Inc.

Chapter 4

AMWA (American Medical Writers Association). (1996). *1996 membership directory*. Bethesda, MD: American Medical Writers Association.

Kelley, P. M., R. E. Masse, T. E. Pearsall, and R. J. Sullivan. (1985). *Academic programs in technical communication: A cooperative effort by the Society for Technical Communication and the Council for Programs in Technical and Scientific Communication*. Washington, DC: Society for Technical Communication, Inc.

Losi, M. J. (1987a). Scientific writing: The servile profession? *AMWA (American Medical Writers Association) Journal* 2(5):16-17.

Losi, M. J. (1987b). 1985-1986 Long-Range Planning Committee report: AMWA membership survey. *AMWA (American Medical Writers Association) Journal* 2(1):13-20.

Pakes, G. E. (1994). Effective application of the team concept to a medical-writing group in a pharmaceutical company. *AMWA (American Medical Writers Association) Journal* 9(3):92-96.

Chapter 5

Accomando, W. P. (1993). CANDA overview: What should a CANDA look like? *Drug Information Journal* 27:407-411.

Alwitt, J., and J. Kinney. (1993). The impact of document image management on clinical data processing. *Drug Information Journal* 27:995-1000.

Hoffman, T. (1996). Document management helps medicines go down: Pharmaceutical firms speed new drug applications to FDA. *Computerworld* 30(24):73.

Lunin, L. F. (1981). Writing and processing drug information in the 80's. *Drug Information Journal* 15:20-24.

Smith, D. L., T. M. Naughton, and R. J. Bonk. (1995). Customized system for electronic publishing: International improvements for document preparation (abstract). Presented at the *Drug Information Association Workshop on International Issues and Perspectives on Medical/Technical Writing and Document Preparation for the Pharmaceutical Industry and Regulatory Agencies*, Philadelphia, PA.

Studebaker, J. F. (1993). Computers in the New Drug Application process. *Journal of Chemical Information and Computer Sciences 33*:86-94.

Warr, W. A. (1991). Some observations on piecemeal electronic publishing solutions in the pharmaceutical industry. *Journal of Chemical Information and Computer Sciences 31*:181-186.

Wasserman, R. S. (1990). Use of an electronic publishing system for production of pharmaceutical product literature. *Drug Information Journal 24*:763-768.

Chapter 6

Food and Drug Law Institute. (1995). *Compilation of Food and Drug Laws, Volume I.* Washington, DC: The Food and Drug Law Institute.

Mannion, J. C., A. Abruzzini, G. Nichoalds, S. Hessenthaler, and C. Uhlinger. (1994). Predictable challenges in the preparation of the clinical sections of NDAs and PLAs. *Applied Clinical Trials 3*(3):68-79.

U.S. Department of Health and Human Services. (1988). *Guideline for the format and content of the clinical and statistical sections of new drug applications.* Washington, DC: Public Health Service, Food and Drug Administration.

Chapter 7

Friedman, L. M., C. D. Furberg, and D. L. DeMets. (1984). *Fundamentals of clinical trials.* See chapter "Reporting and interpretation of results." Littleton, MA: John Wright, PSG Inc.

Nightingale, S. L. (1995). Challenges in international harmonization. *Drug Information Journal 29*:1-9.

U.S. Department of Health and Human Services, Public Health Service, Food and Drug Administration (FDA). (1988). *Guideline for the format and content of the clinical and statistical sections of new drug applications.*

Chapter 8

Spilker, B. (1991). *Guide to clinical trials.* See chapter "Benefit-to-risk assessments and comparisons." New York: Raven Press.

U.S. Department of Health and Human Services. (1987). *Guideline for the format and content of the summary for new drug and antibiotic applications.* Washington, DC: Public Health Service, Food and Drug Administration.

U.S. Department of Health and Human Services. (1988). *Guideline for the format and content of the clinical and statistical sections of new drug applications.* Washington, DC: Public Health Service, Food and Drug Administration.

Chapter 9

U.S. Department of Health and Human Services. (1987). *Guideline for the format and content of the summary for new drug and antibiotic applications.* Washington, DC: Public Health Service, Food and Drug Administration.

U.S. Department of Health and Human Services. (1997). International Conference on Harmonisation; Good Clinical Practice: Consolidated guideline; availability. *Federal Register 62*(90):25692-25709.

Chapter 10

Blake, P., and M. J. Ratcliffe. (1991). Can we accelerate drug development? *Drug Information Journal 24*:13-18.

Bonk, R. J, M. J. Myers, and W. F. McGhan. (1995). Drug expenditures in a balanced strategy for healthcare policy. *PharmacoEconomics 7*(6):534-542.

The Food & Drug Letter. (1994). New computer system may speed drug approval process. *The Food & Drug Letter 462*:1-8.

Chapter 11

International Committee of Medical Journal Editors. (1993). *Uniform Requirements for Manuscripts Submitted to Biomedical Journals and Supplemental Statements from the International Committee of Medical Journal Editors.* Philadelphia: Secretariat Office, American College of Physicians (not covered by copyright).

McLellan, M. F. (1995). Authorship in biomedical publication: "How many people can wield one pen?" *AMWA (American Medical Writers Association) Journal 10*(1):11-13.

Pakes, G. E. (1993). Ensuring quality and timeliness of written medical projects: The role of medical publishing at Glaxo Inc. *AMWA (American Medical Writers Association) Journal 8*(2):50-55.

Severin, W. J., and J. W. Tankard Jr. (1988). *Communication theories: Origins, methods, uses,* Second Edition. See chapter "Perception and communication." New York: Longman Inc.

Chapter 12

Bailar, J. C., III, Chair, for the Editorial Policy Committee. (1990). *Ethics and policy in scientific publication.* Bethesda, MD: Council of Biology Editors.

Day, R. A. (1994). *How to write and publish a scientific paper,* Fourth Edition. Phoenix: Oryx Press.

Gastel, B. (1994). Journal submissions other than scientific papers. In: *Biomedical communication: Selected AMWA workshops,* edited by P. Minick. Bethesda, MD: American Medical Writers Association.

Iles, R. I. (1994). Organizing the scientific journal paper: Guidance on what to write, where, and how. In: *Biomedical communication: Selected AMWA workshops,* edited by P. Minick. Bethesda, MD: American Medical Writers Association.

International Committee of Medical Journal Editors. (1993). *Uniform Requirements for manuscripts submitted to biomedical journals and supplemental statements from the International Committee of Medical Journal Editors.* Philadelphia: Secretariat Office, American College of Physicians (not covered by copyright).

McCann, J. (1990). Working the odds: How to get your manuscript published in the medical journal you want. *AMWA (American Medical Writers Association) Journal* 5(2):6-7.

Rennie, D. (1991). Preface. In: *Peer Review in Scientific Publishing*, edited by Council of Biology Editors, Inc. Chicago: Council of Biology Editors, Inc.

Spilker, B. (1991). *Guide to clinical trials.* See chapter "Preparing articles for publication." New York: Raven Press.

Chapter 13

Day, R. A. (1994a). *How to write and publish a scientific paper,* Fourth Edition. See chapter "How to present a paper orally." Phoenix: Oryx Press.

Day, R. A. (1994b). *How to write and publish a scientific paper,* Fourth Edition. See chapter "How to prepare a poster." Phoenix: Oryx Press.

Day, R. A. (1994c). *How to write and publish a scientific paper,* Fourth Edition. See chapter "How to write a conference report." Phoenix: Oryx Press.

Eastman, J. D., and E. R. Klein. (1991). Conference proceedings: A valuable "checklist" to make publication easier. *AMWA (American Medical Writers Association) Journal* 6(1):21-23.

Eastman, J. D., and E. R. Klein. (1994). Writing abstracts. In: *Biomedical communication: Selected AMWA workshops*, edited by P. Minick. Bethesda, MD: American Medical Writers Association.

Smith, G. M. (1996). *The peer-reviewed journal: A comprehensive guide through the editorial process.* See chapter "Conferences, symposia, and professional meetings." New Orleans: Chatgris Press.

Chapter 14

Krause, J., and H. N. Eldin. (1993). Ethical criteria and pharmaceutical advertising: Comparison of the WHO Ethical Criteria with the IFPMA Code of Pharmaceutical Marketing Practices and the EC Directive on Pharmaceutical Advertising. *Drugs Made in Germany 36*(3):78-90.

Pines, W. L. (1993). *FDA Advertising and Promotion Manual.* Washington, DC: Thompson Publishing Group.

Smith, M. C. (1991). *Pharmaceutical Marketing: Strategies and Cases.* Binghamton, NY: The Haworth Press, Inc.

Spilker, B., and P. Cuatrecasas. (1990). *Inside the drug industry.* See chapter "Marketing activities." Barcelona: JR Prous, SA.

Chapter 15

Angel, J. (1988). Trends in medical publishing: How health care affects the industry. *AMWA (American Medical Writers Association) Journal* 3(3):7-10.

Cox, B. G. (1989). The art of writing patient education materials. *AMWA (American Medical Writers Association) Journal* 4(1):11-14.

Foote, M. A., and J. Flynn. (1993). Biotechnology basics for medical writers. *AMWA (American Medical Writers Association) Journal* 8(3):86-89.

Gray, B. S. (1994). Health communicators as agents of social change. *AMWA (American Medical Writers Association) Journal* 9(1):11-14.

Siegel, J. E., M. C. Weinstein, L. B. Russell, and M. R. Gold (1996) (for the Panel on Cost-Effectiveness in Health and Medicine). Recommendations for reporting cost-effectiveness analyses. *Journal of the American Medical Association* 276(16):1339-1341.

Index

Page numbers followed by the letter "f" indicate figures; those followed by the letter "t" indicate tables.

Order Your Own Copy of
This Important Book for Your Personal Library!

MEDICAL WRITING IN DRUG DEVELOPMENT
A Practical Guide for Pharmaceutical Research

_____ in hardbound at $34.95 (ISBN: 0-7890-0174-8)

_____ in softbound at $19.95 (ISBN: 0-7890-0449-6)

COST OF BOOKS_____	☐ **BILL ME LATER:** ($5 service charge will be added) (Bill-me option is good on US/Canada/Mexico orders only; not good to jobbers, wholesalers, or subscription agencies.)
OUTSIDE USA/CANADA/ MEXICO: ADD 20%_____	
POSTAGE & HANDLING_____ (US: $3.00 for first book & $1.25 for each additional book) Outside US: $4.75 for first book & $1.75 for each additional book)	☐ Check here if billing address is different from shipping address and attach purchase order and billing address information. Signature_____
SUBTOTAL_____	☐ **PAYMENT ENCLOSED: $**_____
IN CANADA: ADD 7% GST_____	☐ **PLEASE CHARGE TO MY CREDIT CARD.**
STATE TAX_____ (NY, OH & MN residents, please add appropriate local sales tax)	☐ Visa ☐ MasterCard ☐ AmEx ☐ Discover ☐ Diner's Club
FINAL TOTAL_____ (If paying in Canadian funds, convert using the current exchange rate. UNESCO coupons welcome.)	Account #_____ Exp. Date_____ Signature_____

Prices in US dollars and subject to change without notice.

NAME _____

INSTITUTION _____

ADDRESS _____

CITY _____

STATE/ZIP _____

COUNTRY _____ COUNTY (NY residents only) _____

TEL _____ FAX _____

E-MAIL_____

May we use your e-mail address for confirmations and other types of information? ☐ Yes   ☐ No

Order From Your Local Bookstore or Directly From
The Haworth Press, Inc.
10 Alice Street, Binghamton, New York 13904-1580 • USA
TELEPHONE: 1-800-HAWORTH (1-800-429-6784) / Outside US/Canada: (607) 722-5857
FAX: 1-800-895-0582 / Outside US/Canada: (607) 772-6362
E-mail: getinfo@haworth.com
PLEASE PHOTOCOPY THIS FORM FOR YOUR PERSONAL USE.

BOF96